Spiritual Life

Spiritual Life

The Foundation for Preaching and Teaching

John H. Westerhoff

 Westminster John Knox Press
Louisville, Kentucky

Scripture quotations from the New Revised Standard Version of the Bible are copyright © 1989 by the Division of Christian Education of the National Council of the Churches of Christ in the U.S.A., and are used by permission.

Book design by Drew Stevens
Cover design by Frank Perrone

First edition

Published by Westminster John Knox Press
Louisville, Kentucky

This book is printed on acid-free paper that meets the American National Standards Institute Z39.48 standard. ∞

PRINTED IN THE UNITED STATES OF AMERICA

94 95 96 97 98 99 00 01 02 03 04 — 10 9 8 7 6 5 4 3 2 1

Library of Congress Cataloging-in-Publication Data

Westerhoff, John H., date.
    Spiritual life : the foundation for preaching and teaching / John
H. Westerhoff. — 1st ed.
        p.   cm.
    ISBN 0-664-25500-0 (alk. paper)
    1. Preaching.   2. Spiritual life.   I. Title.
BV4211.2.W432   1994
248.8'92—dc20   94-10408

Dedicated to Caroline,
my wife,
best friend,
and spiritual companion

Contents

Preface

This small book for those who preach or teach, laypersons and clergy, has been writing itself for some time. Almost a decade ago, I sensed the need for academic courses in both spirituality and spiritual formation at Duke University Divinity School. At first this concern was shared by only a few students and faculty. Courses in spirituality were seriously questioned. Today, spiritual formation is a major concern of faculty and students. More than ten courses offered by six faculty members are among the most highly recommended and popular courses in the curriculum. Realizing the crucial importance of spirituality for preachers and teachers, Duke now has an endowed program in spirituality unequaled in any school of its kind.

During this same period, I discovered that laity and clergy across the country were more interested in my lecturing on issues related to the spiritual life than in any other subject in pastoral theology. For example, my course on "Spirituality and Preaching" at the College of Preachers in Washington, D.C., was always filled early and oversubscribed. Indeed, this book is based on material presented in that course. Also, the most popular event in 1993 at the Institute of Pastoral Studies was "The Church School Teacher and the Spiritual Life."

More important, I learned in my own experience the need for a maturing spiritual life. A few years ago, a crisis in my life led me to realize that even though I had a spiritual discipline and had been teaching spirituality, my personal spiritual life was in disarray. As a result, while continuing to teach, I became an associate of the Society of St. John the Evangelist, an Anglo-Catholic men's religious order. I lived with and shared in the spiritual life of the brothers at St. John's House in Durham, North Carolina. That experience, along with a number of directed retreats, proved to be transforming in my life.

This experience led me further to realize that if I was to teach pastoral theology, I needed to get back into the parish. I also had a dream of birthing an Institute for Pastoral Studies housed in a parish, to provide an educational resource for laity and clergy. Two years ago, after my marriage to Caroline Hughes, onetime senior consultant with the Alban Institute in Washington, D.C., and now the bishop's canon for education in the Episcopal Diocese of Atlanta, I moved to Atlanta and was invited to house my institute at St. Bartholomew's Episcopal Church. In order to do that, I entered into a part-time teaching relationship with Duke. Once again, I learned that the greatest concern and interest of laity and clergy was spirituality. For example, a series I conducted for parents of young children that attracted great interest included sessions on "Parents as Teachers and Preachers" and on "The Spirituality of Parenthood."

When the rector of St. Bartholomew's left to become the dean of a cathedral, I was called to become the interim rector for a year. I accepted and took a year's leave of absence from Duke. While on this leave, as interim rector of St. Bartholomew's Episcopal Church in Atlanta, I became increasingly convinced that the spiritual life is at the heart of my life as a teacher and preacher, indeed, essential to a faithful ministry.

During this period, while continuing my work with the institute, I became increasingly aware that many clergy begin a renewed quest for greater faithfulness in their vocation when they recognize a condition within themselves that they call "burn-out." They realize they have nothing left to inform their teaching and preaching. They therefore attempt to meet this need by returning to the seminary for continuing education in the theological disciplines. While such academic work is vital and does help for a time, it ultimately does not heal their disease. Typically, they next define the problem as "drain-out." Having worked too many hours a day and too many days a week, they resolve to go on a vacation. This break also helps them, but soon they discover that they need another and another. Finally, if they have not given up, and some regretfully do, they realize that their foundational problem is "rust-out." That is, all that has given shape and form to their lives as preachers and teachers is eroding. Their spiritual lives have been ignored. Only when they come to this point are they ready to take the radical step necessary to make their spiritual lives the focus of their attention. Having done so, they discover that their preaching and teaching take on a character and quality they have never known before. They once again feel refreshed and have something about which to preach and teach.

However, this book is not solely for clergy, or even clergy and those professionals responsible for the church's educational ministry. This book is for volunteer church-school teachers who each week proclaim the gospel in word and example as well as strive, through instruction and reflection on experience, to help themselves and their students understand the implications of that gospel for their daily lives.

I have learned that our work as teachers and preachers is never completed, it is not easy to evaluate, and its demands are constant. We have little choice about whom we work with; our work drains our energy; it produces stress; and we live in a society that works against and does not appreciate our efforts. Unless our identity is hid in God, we will never know what to do, let alone survive in doing it. We must become persons of prayer. Prayer is paying attention. Without that single-minded attention to God, we will rarely hear anything worth repeating, catch a vision worth asking others to gaze upon, or have anything worth mounting a pulpit to proclaim. If we do not pray, our work will become drudgery rather than vocation, a meaningless round of activities rather than ministry.

Therefore, before beginning a new chapter in my life as a priest on the staff of St. Luke's Episcopal Church in Atlanta, I felt I needed to write this small book, which I hope will prove a practical, inspirational book for anyone who teaches or preaches, lay or clergy, from any Christian tradition. My intent in doing so is to provide a resource on the spiritual life that may aid us to experience a rebirth in the vitality and faithfulness in our ministry as the church's preachers and teachers. I envision this book as being a gift for church-school teachers at their installation, for seminarians, for men and women before their ordination, for directors of Christian education, and for all clergy.

In the first chapter, "Exploring the Spiritual Life," I describe the nature and character of the spiritual life over time. In the second chapter, "Preaching and Teaching in a New Day," I discuss why the time in which we live requires new understandings of how we preach and teach, as well as explain the significance of the spiritual life in preaching and teaching. Chapter 3, "The Spirituality of Preachers and Teachers," explores the special spiritual qualities needed by preachers and teachers, and the following chapter, "The Spirituality of Preaching and Teaching," explores in what ways spirituality can inform us about preaching and teaching. Chapter 5, "Various Ways of Living Spiritually," describes the vast variety of ways in which people can live the spiritual life.

The final chapter, "Developing a Spiritual Discipline," explains how a preacher or teacher goes about developing this aspect of her or his life.

Much of what is here I owe to others. It is what I have chosen to hear and read during my own quest. I trust that I have been faithful in how I have used their more seminal work. I, of course, hold myself responsible for the thoughts offered. I also acknowledge the great many and growing number of fine books on the spiritual life, but I trust that this short, easy-to-read book, which has emerged from my life experience as a teacher and preacher, will find a somewhat unique place among the others. I hope that you, the reader, find that to be true.

In any case, thank you for choosing to read and reflect on my thoughts. Writing them has been helpful to me; I can only pray that it will have helped you to ponder them.

Acknowledgments

The material in this book is based on lectures given by John Westerhoff during a conference, "The Spirituality of Preaching," held at the College of Preachers in the spring of 1992. The College of Preachers, located on the grounds of the National Cathedral in Washington, D.C., is an interdenominational center of continuing education dedicated to strengthening, sustaining, and nourishing those who are called to the ministry of preaching. In its sixty-eight-year history, the college has served over eighteen thousand clergy and laity through its conferences and Fellows and Readers programs.

Grateful acknowledgment is made to Harcourt Brace & Company for permission to reprint "Sunday School, circa 1950" from *Revolutionary Petunias & Other Poems,* by Alice Walker. Copyright © 1970 by Alice Walker.

1

Exploring the Spiritual Life

The spiritual life, as I understand it, is ordinary, everyday life lived in an ever-deepening and loving relationship to God and therefore to one's true or healthy self, all people, and the whole of creation.

The spiritual life—"Love the Lord your God with all your heart, and with all your soul, and with all your mind, and with all your strength"—and the moral life—"Love your neighbor as yourself"—are directly related (see Mark 12:30–31). The spiritual life, however, is prior to the moral life, for we can love the neighbor as God loves us only if first we have experienced that love affair with God. More important, we cannot love God except in response to God's love for us.

This love affair with God is the one and only end of human life. All else is means. It was for this relationship that we were created and have our being. Because this axiom is true, nothing and no one can take away from us the meaning and purpose of our lives. Indeed, the justification for all other relationships and actions is that they enhance and enliven this relationship with God.

Yet we have a paradox. The test of the character and quality of our relationship with God is measured by the character and quality of all other relationships. It would simply be false to say that our relationship with God is going well while we are exhibiting prejudiced behavior, nursing anger, or allowing estrangements. It would be more honest and true to say that if I cannot forgive a particular person, then my relationship with God is troubled.

The central theme of Kenneth Leech's work over the years has been the essential unity of Christian spirituality and Christian social and political commitment. With him, I am convinced that a renewed Christian spirituality will be a spirituality of justice and peace, but I am also convinced that any faithful striving for justice and peace will emerge from the life of prayer. In his latest and perhaps most important book, *The Eye of the Storm: Living Spiritually in the Real World,* Leech writes, "I have come to see, as an activist, the central place of silence in my life and in the lives of all who would work for peace and justice at more than the surface level."[1]

In a similar vein, I heard Pope John XXIII comment in a homily, "Let no one imagine there is any difference between perfection of the soul and the business of life. We are not to abandon the world in order to achieve perfection."

The spiritual life is not to be contrasted with the material life. Such dualisms as spiritual and material, sacred and secular, personal and social, cultic life and daily life, prayer and action are not acceptable. All life is spiritual, but that spiritual life has two dimensions, namely, a material dimension and a nonmaterial dimension, an objective and subjective character.

All life is sacramental, that is, it has both an outward, visible and an inward, hidden dimension. As such, it is comprised of both a secular character, which is rational, immanent, this-worldly, material, political, and human, and a sacred character, which is prerational, nonmaterial, transcendent, otherworldly, pietistic, and divine.

All of life is communal in that it has a personal dimension and a social dimension, which are comprised of an inner and an outer journey respectively. Human life ought never to be considered individualistic or privatistic, because it involves both private and group prayer, an interior and an exterior life, contemplation and action.

All of life is liturgical, that is, it is comprised of two dimensions, namely, cultic or ritual life and daily life. Like all dimensions of reality, these two are directly related to and affect each other. As in our love of God and love of neighbor, the value of our rituals and devotional life is judged by how we behave in our daily life and work. This relationship of ritual and daily life explains why in the history of the church, when it was concluded that the church was not being as faithful as it should, there was a movement to reform its worship.

A healthy human rhythm is comprised of an oscillation between maintaining a subconscious reliance on God's presence and action and giving conscious attention to God's presence and action. In the first instance, we are involved with other human beings in daily life and work. In the second, we intentionally look to God so that God might convert, nurture, and send us back into the world to live more faithfully.

One way to describe this movement between these two dimensions of life is to imagine a child sitting on a parent's lap in the park. When the child feels loved and secure, the child ventures off to play. Eventually, the child gets tired, has a confrontation, becomes lonely, or suffers a mishap and runs back to jump into the parent's arms to be comforted and then, once again after the experience of love and security, returns to play. So it is that the human life of prayer, the means by which we maintain and manifest our spiritual life, is a movement between prayer as devotional life and prayer as daily life and work.

Images of God

The health of our spiritual life is also directly related to our image of God. One of my favorite parables is that of the talents (Matt. 25:14–29). In the parable, the master of a house entrusts his servants with his property before he sets out on a journey. To one he gives five talents; to another, two; and to the third, one. Then he leaves them. The first two servants double what was entrusted to them, and when the master (God) returns, he praises them for being trustworthy. When the third, having hidden the talent entrusted to him because he feared the master, returns that one talent, the master of the house condemns him for his behavior.

While many have interpreted this parable in terms of stewardship, I suggest a much more radical and subversive interpretation. Let us suppose that the first two characters are what we call in literature "throwaway characters." That is, they are included in the story to heighten our awareness of and draw a contrast with a third person. Now in this particular parable, each person has a perception of God and God's nature and character. Recall that when their master (God) returns, the first two report what they have done, expecting that the master will be pleased. They have acted on their perceptions of God, and God praises them. However, the third explains, "I perceived that you were a harsh, demanding, critical parent, which I hope helps you understand why I did what I did." And God responds, "You perceive that I am a harsh, demanding, critical parent? Well, in that case, I will take from you what I entrusted to you and give it to the others who perceived me as generous, forgiving, and loving and then cast you into a place where there is gnashing of teeth."

This parable about faith or perception confronts us with the subversive contention that the only God we are able to experience is the God we image. That is an awesome thought. Many people have images of a god that are not of God but a distortion of God. For such persons, a healthy spiritual life is impossible. It is therefore very important that we be sure that our images of God and God's nature and character are faithful to the gospel.

We also need to be sure that our spiritual life is not hampered by the absence of feminine images of God. Without such images our spiritual life will be flawed. The great spiritual writers throughout history were aware of that and therefore imaged a God who had both masculine and feminine characteristics. They often metaphorically spoke of God as mother and father. It is because many people are unaware of this literature, penned by both men and women, that masculine images of God have been defended as normative. Recall, for example, how Julian of Norwich referred to Jesus as her sister. Recall also how Jesus used feminine images for the God he called Father and in his lament over Jerusalem cried, "How often have I desired to gather your children together as a hen gathers her brood under her wings, and you were not willing" (Matt. 23:37). Building on that feminine image, my favorite centering prayer has become, "Gentle loving God, the mother of my soul, hold me as your own."

Theologically, there is a paradox concerning this God with whom we are to relate. The creed begins, "We believe in one God, the Father, the Almighty, maker of heaven and earth, of all that is, seen and unseen." The God to whom we give our loyalty and love is a majestic, transcendent mystery, one whom we can never know fully and, indeed, know only through God's self-revelation. But this same God is an immanent, loving parent with whom we can have an intimate friendship. Thus acknowledging that we can never know fully this friend and that our friend must reveal him- or herself to us, friendship may be our best metaphor for understanding the spiritual life, our relationship with God.

God as Friend

Aristotle describes three kinds of friendships: friendships based on the pleasure another gives us; friendships based on another's usefulness to us; and friendships based on a shared love of the good, the true, and the beautiful. Aristotle defends the last as the sort of friendship required for the moral life. It is this same understanding of friendship that is necessary for a spiritual friendship with God if it is to lead to the moral life God desires. That is, righteousness, a right relationship with God, is dependent on our commitment to abide in God's reign, that condition in which God's will is known and done. As Paul Wadell contends in his book *Friendship and the Moral Life*, friendship that aims at life in God's reign where agape love flourishes is the means to life in God's reign where agape love is normative.[2] Agape, universal, undeserved love for all, is learned through the development of a friendship with God founded on a shared love of the good, the true, and the beautiful.

By applying the metaphor of friendship to our relationship with God, we discover that we already know a great deal about the nature and character of the spiritual life as well as how that life grows and matures as a result of the successes and failures we have experienced in human friendships.

Consider the following: It is difficult to develop an intimate friendship with someone unless we spend a significant amount of quality time with that person. Would we develop much of a friendship with someone if we spent only one or two hours a week or what amounts to about four days a year with her or him? Why is it, then, that we wonder why our relationship with God is not as good as we desire when we spend quality time with God only for a few hours each week, mostly on Sunday mornings? Our relationship with God is directly related to the amount and quality of time we spend consciously with God daily.

Friendships require that we share emotions freely, but many people attempt to hide their emotions from God. The psalmist has no difficulty telling God that he will be happy if God dashes his enemy's children against the rocks (Psalm 137). That is how the psalmist felt and he expressed it. I suspect, however, that the psalmist never believed that God would do what he suggested. Nevertheless, he surely must have felt better for expressing honestly the emotions he was experiencing.

Indeed, there is a spiritual exercise for dealing with disordered affections in which, through our imaginations, we take someone before God and act out in words and deeds all our feelings about that person until we have emptied them from our hearts and minds. Then, in the silence that follows, we are to open ourselves so God can fill with God's love the empty space that exists. Still too many of us have difficulty acknowledging our emotions and feelings, let alone expressing them, to God. We would be healthier and our friendship with God more intimate if we did. Just as I worry about those couples who say they never argue or express anger with each other (do they really care about each other?), I worry about those who cannot even imagine swearing at God. Do they love God enough to be angry with God?

Further, in the world of friendships, we do not develop much of a relationship if we do all the talking. There are many people who confess that they have never heard God say anything. If they treated people the way they treat God, people would not say anything to them either. Every time they pray they talk and never listen.

There is nothing wrong with vocal prayer, but we need to combine it with silence so God can communicate with us. I say "communicate," for rarely does God speak to us with words. God speaks to us through interior emotions, dreams, visions, intuitions, and the like. Of course, we need to acknowledge that many of us were socialized to distrust or ignore our feelings and intuitions. Thinking was all that was important. But God speaks to us through our feelings, our hearts. Only then do we use our minds to understand what our hearts have heard.

The Christian spiritual life is grounded in a very specific image of God, namely, a personal God who encounters us in love. Prayer is that personal love relationship between God and ourselves initiated by God. Prayer is our awareness of the movement of God toward us in which we open our hearts, minds, and wills to God by first listening and then responsively moving toward God so that we might grow in that relationship.

Friendships also require that we share common activities that give us mutual joy. If one person is not at all interested in what another wants to do or joins the other in an activity only to please the other, that relationship is on shaky ground. Likewise, if the only way we will maintain the relationship is if the other person agrees to do what we enjoy, the relationship will not endure. A healthy friendship includes sharing activities enjoyed by both. The question is: What are you and God working on together that gives both of you pleasure and satisfaction?

Friendships take time to cultivate. In the beginning they require attention and hard work, but if later we continually try too hard to control the relationship, it will fail. This observation has implications for the spiritual pilgrimage that I will describe shortly. My main point, however, is that we have an analogue for the spiritual life in our experience with human friendships and therefore need to use that knowledge in furthering the development of our spiritual lives.

The Fruit of the Spirit

Typically people ask, Are there any clues to whether or not I am growing spiritually? Paul suggests there is one test, namely, growth in the fruit of the Spirit: "The fruit of the Spirit is love, joy, peace, patience, kindness, generosity, faithfulness, gentleness, and self-control" (Gal. 5:22–23). So often people erroneously read this text as if it says "fruits." It really describes a single fruit comprised of numerous characteristics. Our spiritual life is improving when all of these dimensions of a single fruit are present. Indeed, to have one dimension of the fruit without the others turns that fruit into a distortion. For example, to have only patience and not the other characteristics can lead to the vice of complacence. But if patience is added to the others—love, joy, peace, kindness, generosity, faithfulness, gentleness, and self-control—then patience becomes a virtue.

So it is that this one fruit of the Spirit is described in many ways. The fruit is love, that sense of being loved and lovable which results in a sense of self-worth and makes possible loving those who act in unlovable ways. It is an awareness that we are all recovering sinners, accepted though unacceptable, and loved undeservedly.

The fruit is joy, that sense of well-being which comes from experiences of redemption, experiences in which God turns negatives into positives. It results in a conviction that we can trust God and that with God, all things are possible.

The fruit is peace, that sense of centeredness and well-being which results from being reconciled with God, self, others, and creation. It is that awareness that nothing can separate us from the love of God and that therefore the meaning and purpose of our lives will be fulfilled.

The fruit of the spirit is patience, that willingness to neither resist nor run from life. It is that ability to be present to life with a calm composure that waits and watches for God.

The fruit is kindness, that is, the ability to be present to others in compassionate, caring ways that, while we may not like them or their behavior, seek their good no matter what the cost to ourselves.

The fruit is generosity, that ability to be liberal in giving of ourselves and our possessions which comes from an awareness that all that we are and have are gifts entrusted to us by a generous and loving God.

The fruit is gentleness, that quiet approach to people and all of life which sees the image of God in them, including those who distort and deny it. Having no desire to make others into our image, we make it possible for them to discover the truth about themselves, namely, that they have been created in God's image.

The fruit is self-control, that inner directedness which comes from the life of prayer and frees us to be controlled by God and do the will of God freely.

A Pilgrimage

As we explore the various experiences that persons have as they focus their attention on their relationship with God, two primary kinds of experiences emerge, namely, the pietistic and the mystic. The pietistic emphasizes immediate, affective experiences of God and assurance of divine election. It typically comes in the form of a single, dramatic, emotional conversion experience. The mystic, by contrast, emphasizes a long, slow journey into a union with God through spiritual exercises. It is a pilgrimage comprised of a series of conversion and nurturing experiences (the first often being dramatic and memorable because it was the first) into an ever-deepening and loving relationship with God. This second kind of experience is often misunderstood as something we accomplish through our efforts at prayer. It is rather better understood as the way that God has designed for us to cooperate with God in making possible the relationship God desires. Insofar as I have never experienced the pietistic way, I will attempt to describe briefly the mystic, which I know best.

Most spiritual writers describe this spiritual pilgrimage as beginning in adulthood. I offer here, however, some broad descriptions of the earlier years based on my own experience. Remember, this pilgrimage proceeds only if aided and can be arrested at any point if persons see no reason to continue and choose to bring the pilgrimage to a close.

In the beginning, the spiritual life may appear childish, but it is natural and experiential. Persons identify with their parents or a community and their prayer life is imitative and verbal. More important, many young children have significant experiences of God, but because they are not able to name, describe, explain, or understand them until they are much older, we are apt to conclude that they have none. Further, we often forget that children are able to engage in that intuitive way of thinking and knowing which is at the heart of the spiritual life.

As persons develop their intellectual way of thinking and knowing, they tend to move toward a more reflective period in their spiritual life. Typically, they experience doubt about God's presence and action in their lives. Having given up their innocence and childishness, they may experience difficulty in relating to God. Their prayer life either remains rote prayer or dries up. For a while, the quest for God through the intellect is satisfying and necessary, but eventually it leads to despair. Now they are ready to become childlike and integrate the intuitive way of knowing into the intellectual way and, with God's help and the Spirit's leading, move into the next stage of the spiritual pilgrimage.

At this point we can use the insights of those who have written about the spiritual pilgrimage throughout history. The insights I have found most helpful result from analogies used by Teresa of Avila and her spiritual friend John of the Cross. In her autobiography, Teresa discusses the life of prayer. She images the soul as God's garden, planted by God and belonging to God. The water by which the flowers in the garden are nourished and brought to maturity is our life of prayer or, better, our experience of God in prayer. The flowers represent the outcomes of this life of prayer, this watering of the garden with water God provides, namely, the virtuous life exemplified by the fruit of the Spirit.

Teresa, therefore, describes the beginning of our adult spiritual pilgrimage as being like drawing water from a deep well with a long rope and small can and then carrying it a long distance to where our garden has been planted. That is, the spiritual life in the beginning is simply difficult, hard work from our human point of view. Prayer is a highly disciplined activity. It is labor-intensive and often without a great deal to show for it.

While we may have experiences of consolation, we also have those of desolation. God's Spirit draws us toward God, and the evil spirit, disguised as God's Spirit, entices us to move away from God. Nevertheless, if we faithfully discern between the spirits and are faithful in our striving toward an ever deeper and more loving relationship with God, then we find, to return to Teresa's analogy, that there is a waterwheel that makes it possible to draw water from the well more easily. Now we need only to collect the water and carry it to our garden, where growth begins to appear. At this point we will continue to experience good and bad days, but the bad days will be understandable while, in general, our prayer life will appear rich and our relationship with God satisfying.

Then, Teresa explains, the well goes dry. We experience the absence of God and nothing we have done in the past helps us. John of the Cross describes this experience as the first dark night, the dark night of the senses. That is, all our past successful efforts at prayer, our spiritual discipline, fail us. It is as if God were saying to us, You have manipulated this relationship long enough. Now you are going to have to wait until I decide to contact you.

For those who are willing to give up their striving, wait patiently, and watch expectantly, God returns in a beautiful way. As Teresa explains it, a spring appears as a gift. All we need to do is dig an irrigation ditch to our garden. Our experiences of consolation are more frequent and intense, but our experiences of desolation appear to last longer and are more intense also as the struggle between God's Spirit and the evil spirit intensifies. Nevertheless, our prayer life has become a more natural part of our lives. We experience being able to give ourselves to God more completely and enjoy God's presence more fully.

Then the bottom drops out, and we are devastated. All of our hopes and our faith and our prayers seem to be in vain. John says we then experience a second dark night, the dark night of the soul. What is now demanded is that we give up all our striving, all our attempts at control, and simply float. If we do, a gentle rain, as Teresa images it, appears and our garden becomes a rain forest. Now we live in union with God. Our spiritual life is made perfect or whole, and our moral life reveals it. All of life is a prayer, and we are praying without ceasing.

Now, while such allegorical attempts to describe our spiritual pilgrimage can be helpful, everyone experiences the journey in her or his own way. What is important is that we are on the pilgrimage and willing to do what is necessary to grow into an ever-deepening and loving relationship with God.

2

Preaching and Teaching in a New Day

As the title of this book suggests, I believe that the spiritual life is the foundation for preaching and teaching. In this chapter I explore my understanding of preaching and teaching and why I believe that the historical context in which we live necessitates a new spiritual approach to both.

The didache is that part of the gospel teaching directed toward Christian character, that is, Christian identity and way of life. The kerygma is that part of the gospel proclamation directed toward the transmission of the sacred story that is foundational to Christian faith and makes possible the Christian way of life. While at times there have been attempts to understand didache and kerygma, teaching and preaching, as two distinct entities, most would agree that they are simply two dimensions of a single entity. There can be no separation of that sacred narrative which informs how we perceive life and our lives and the way of life which emanates from that perception.

In Matthew's account of God's good news, we read, "Then Jesus went about all the cities and villages, teaching in their synagogues, and proclaiming the good news of the kingdom, and curing every disease and every sickness" (Matt. 9:35). In the gospel narrative, both preaching—heralding the Christian certainties of the faith—and teaching—revealing the significance of these certainties for life and our lives—are essential for the Christian life of faith, a life that necessarily combines word and action. It is important, therefore, that while we may consider them separately, we keep preaching and teaching in conversation with each other.

Preaching and Teaching

In the summer of 1993, David Buttrick delivered a lecture sponsored by the College of Preachers in Washington, D.C., on the occasion of the installation of its new president and warden. Buttrick made a point that many others have been making, namely, that we live in a time of transition. The era of the Enlightenment is drawing to a close, and a new era is beginning to emerge.

One sign of the times to which he pointed was the significant change that has, over time, been occurring in our language, a change similar to the alterations in language that accompanied the fall of the Greco-Roman Empire and the collapse of the medieval synthesis. He pointed out that while new scientific words have been added, the overall number of words in our language has been shrinking and, more significantly, our language has been becoming increasingly abstract.

Buttrick asserted also that human consciousness has been changing. That is, today we understand our world differently than did people at other times in history. Enlightenment art, he commented, was painted from a third-person perspective, as if by an objective observer. But painting and sculpture, which now, as always, offer early insights into cultural and historical change, have radically changed in the modern period. For example, art now appears to be painted from several different perspectives at once.

Buttrick went on to contend that most Anglican, Roman Catholic, and mainline Protestant sermons, like Enlightenment paintings, are still being delivered in a third person, objective, abstract style. Typically, these sermons are static in design. They unpack biblical passages from the perspective of the historical-critical method. They employ abstract theological language and make logical, categorical points related to a single topic. The result, he concluded, is that half of our listeners have become either crypto-fundamentalists or have not been affected by our preaching.

Our preaching, he asserted, must change, as preaching has in other periods of history, if it is to engage contemporary consciousness. We must begin to search for the metaphors, the images, and the strategies that will make the Christian life of faith meaningful for human beings in our era. Buttrick's observations are supported by others who have made similar contentions about teaching.

Teaching faces the same challenge. We have, during this same period, become increasingly concerned with the transmission of information and training in skills. We have become enamored of computerized instruction and behavioral modification. The "back to basics" movement in Christian education has emphasized the acquisition of abstract knowledge about beliefs and behaviors, the memorization of "facts," and obedience to authority.

Few have questioned this approach and its potential to create magna cum laude atheists who know all about Christianity but do not intend to be Christians or who become unthinking, unimaginative followers of authority figures.

Changing Emphases

The importance of the shifts that are occurring in our understandings of reality was made graphically clear to me one day as my wife and I were walking the beach looking for shells. I noticed that when you comb the beach in one direction, you may discover some valuable and beautiful shells but you totally miss others. These others can be found only when you comb the same piece of beach from the opposite direction. I also observed that most people walk in one direction looking for shells and then return with their heads held high, as if there were no others to be found. This insight has an important implication for our conversations about preaching and teaching. We must be careful, when faced with a new world situation, not to cast out all the wisdom of the old world in a search to be relevant, as was often done in the past.

Two and a half centuries ago, a struggle emerged within the faculty of the St. Thomas School in Leipzig. Involving the school's cantor, Johann Sebastian Bach, and its rector, Johann August Ernesti, it was a conflict between the intellectual and intuitional modes of consciousness, between the arts and the sciences. Between the two men was played out the tragic conflict between the artist, one of the last representatives of the Age of Faith, and the younger protagonist of the Age of Reason. Ernesti wished to make the study of scripture and theology the dominant purpose of the school. Bach defended the role of musical expression and the position that the biblical text was designed to release within the reader an intense sort of spiritual activity, faith. Ernesti and his rationalistic, analytical, intellectual perspective finally won the day. The outcome of this conflict dramatizes the birth of a new era that has to this day dominated our culture.

This modern era has realized the inadequacy of conceiving reality in terms of dualisms such as spiritual and material reality. However, in its striving to eliminate such dualisms, it created a monism, namely, that the only reality is objective, material reality because only it can be observed, studied, and understood. Those who wanted to maintain a spiritual reality tended to reestablish the old dualism.

Today, most agree that the era of the Enlightenment has reached its moral limits and necessarily is drawing to a close.

And many do so with some sadness. The light of the Enlightenment was really light: modern science, medicine, and technology are its offspring. It aided us in understanding the scriptures better than ever before; it aided us in reflecting theologically on life and in making rational moral decisions; and it provided us with a historical consciousness. But it also led to the unfortunate conclusion that we could comprehend all of life and control our own destiny. It encouraged us to turn the world, both people and nature, into objects for our analysis and manipulation. And it led us to neglect faith, character, and consciousness.

Andrew Louth, in his amazing book *Discerning the Mystery: An Essay on the Nature of Theology*,[1] writes of what C. S. Lewis called a "dissociation of sensibilities" that began with the seventeenth-century Enlightenment. During these three centuries, the sciences and the arts, theology and spirituality slowly became separated and eventually estranged. Thought about God no longer was related to the movement of the heart toward God. The humanities followed the lead of the sciences in searching for objective truth, and the arts were ignored. In the modern period, Hans-Georg Gadamer and others have attempted to free the humanities from the lure of the historical-critical method; Michael Polanyi and others have attempted to assert that the tacit way of knowing and intuition were closer to reality than the literal and the intellectual.

To be Christian, Louth contends, is not simply to believe something, to have heard or learned something, but to be someone who participates in a community where the mystery of faith is experienced. The Christian tradition, he continues, is not an abstract message but a practice; not a body of doctrine that can be preached about and taught about but a way of life.

Louth maintains that tradition is not another source for doctrine alongside scripture but another way of speaking about the spirit, the inner life of the church, that life in which the Christian is perfected into the image in which we humans were created.

Preaching, Louth continues, needs to be seen in the context of liturgy, something we participate in, not just with our intellects but with all that we are. Liturgy has the power to introduce us to a context and involve us in an action that goes beyond our speaking and aids us to enter the world of silence. All knowledge is tacit. It is not simply objective. It is grasped by a person; it is personal knowing. Our knowledge is more a personal orientation toward reality than any kind of objective account of it. All knowledge of God is rooted in this tacit dimension, best interpreted as silence, the silence of presence, the presence of God who gives God's self to the soul who waits on God in silence.

Louth explains that understanding a literary work, for example, is not a matter of acquiring a conceptual under-standing that is to be the same for everyone. It is rather a matter of experience that takes place in one's engagement with the work and the resulting experience that brings personal understanding and insight for each reader.

We have reached the end of an era of retarded conscious-ness. We have lost or forgotten the experience of a personal God who is present and active in our lives, an awareness that is at the heart of the Christian life of faith. We have neglected the most basic expression of our humanness: prayer. As the British Roman Catholic philosopher Baron von Hügel con-cluded, "Prayer is the essential element of life." The current bankruptcy in our spiritual lives is not solely a misplaced, singular concern for the intellectual way of thinking and knowing, but rather it is an actual denial and neglect of the intuitional way of thinking and knowing. Having placed our attention on theology as doctrine or propositional truth, we have neglected faith, or how we perceive life and our lives. Having focused our attention on ethics as moral decision making, we have neglected character, the person we are and how we are disposed to behave. Having placed our concern on objective experience, we have neglected subjective consciousness. We have gone too far in asserting one-half of the truth, and we need to reestablish that which was lost.

We are not faced with an either-or proposition. We must never neglect the intellectual way of thinking and knowing as we have the intuitional. The significative, conceptual, and analytical aspects of life need to be maintained even as we rediscover the symbolic, mythical, imaginative, and emotive aspects of life.

Nevertheless, we do need to rediscover that mystery is not something about which we can know nothing but that about which we cannot know everything. We need to shift our perception from the God who is total mystery, the one who is majestic and unknowable, to the God who is loving parent and friend. We need to turn from abstract theological concepts about God to narrative, poetry, and song. We need a new awareness of the visual, the artistic, imaginative, associative, and relational activities of the mind. For too long we have been living in the prosaic world of surface reality. We need to shift our attention from theological reflection to spirituality, from discursive prose to poetry, from reason to the imagination, from instruction to formation, from the sciences to the arts.

The imagination is foundational to the spiritual life. If we are to be open to the presence and action of God in our lives and history, we have to live a life of imagination. The imagination is not a human "faculty" but a posture of the whole person toward experience. The fact that religious experience is considered so uncommon does not mean that God is not present and active but that we have made so little of the imagination. A human being as a spiritual being is one who is in the world as one who images.

It was Jacob Burkhardt, the historian, who said that religion without the imagination would become either magic or sentimentality. "He is right," comments Urban Holmes in his book *Ministry and the Imagination*, "because religion that has no sense of the immediate presence of God either attempts to conjure up that presence by human cunning or reduces piety to nostalgia and being 'sweet.'"[2]

We humans are not creatures who think only analytically and logically; we think intuitively and imaginatively. That is, we can "see" the deeper meaning of our experience, as opposed to merely looking on the surface. Preaching and teaching need to move into this intuitive mode if we are to speak or explore the reality of God present and active in our lives.

It would be helpful, therefore, for us to remember that the arts provide us with a unique way of thinking and knowing, a way particularly important to the spiritual life. In that regard, Thomas Merton, the monk, once commented on a dream of Karl Barth, the theologian. Barth loved Mozart's music. He would spend hours listening to Mozart before working on his theological system. But it was Mozart who had commented that the problem with Protestants (such as Barth) was that they were too heady and intellectual. Now as the story goes, Barth had a dream in which he was in heaven and called on to examine Mozart on his theology. He wanted to make it as easy as possible, so all of his questions were about Mozart's masses. But in the dream Mozart refused to respond. Barth could not understand the dream, but Merton suggested that God was trying to tell him that he would be saved more by the music lover in him than by the theologian in him.

The arts provide us with a way of being and living. We do

not judge art, it judges us. We must approach it as we would a person, in a spirit of openness and dialogue. Art requires that we engage it as a subject to be talked with, not about, and never fully comprehended.

Amos Wilder, a man before his time, New Testament scholar and poet, in his seminal work *Theopoetic: Theology and the Religious Imagination* writes, "Religious communication generally must overcome a long addiction to the discursive, the rationalistic, and the prosaic. And the Christian imagination must come halfway to meet the new dreams, mystiques, and mythologies that are gestating in our time."[3] Wilder continues:

> My plea for a theopoetic means doing more justice to the role of the symbol and the pre-rational in the way we deal with experience. We should recognize that human nature and human societies are more deeply motivated by images and fabulations than by ideas. This is where the power lies and the future is shaped.[4]

Edward Robinson, the director of the Center for Spirituality and the Arts at Oxford University, discusses in his book *The Language of Mystery* what he refers to as the enemies of art, namely, imitation and rhetoric.[5] Imitative art results from people asking questions such as: What is this a picture of? What is this poet trying to say? What is that dance or piece of music about? Such questions assume that a work of art is to convey information and make something already known clearer. Such art is imitative art. It neglects the purpose of art, which, as I believe the artist Paul Klee once explained, is not to reproduce the visible but to make visible. The purpose of art is to open us to that which is hidden, to break open a mystery. Imitative art can never do that. Too many teachers want to teach people only that which is self-evident. Too many preachers want to tell people only what they already know.

Further, art that employs rhetoric or the techniques of persuasion is not really art. Few sermons ever reach the level of art in that they are more concerned to put over a point than to help people form one of their own. Few classes ever reach the level of art in that they are more concerned to convince people that something is true than to help them discover the truth.

Parker Palmer, in *To Know As We Are Known,* reflects on the first sin as described in the story of the Fall in Genesis. The problem, writes Palmer, was that Adam and Eve hungered for knowledge that distrusts and excludes God, a knowledge that would put them in control. They longed for that way of thinking and knowing which is at the foundation of the intellectual tradition, a tradition that turns all reality, including people, into objects for our investigation, analysis, and manipulation.[6] In this tradition, we study rather than pray the scriptures. We turn Holy Scripture into an object for our investigation, rather than a subject intended to engage us.

Spiritual reading or praying of the scriptures is different from academic reading or study of the scriptures. In praying scripture, we engage the imagination; in studying scripture, we engage the power of reason. In praying, we involve ourselves subjectively; in studying, we investigate objectively. In praying, we dwell with; in studying, we dig into. In praying, we are docile and stand under the text; in studying, we are dialectical and stand above the text. In praying, we treat the text dynamically and relate it directly to our life story; in studying, we dissect the text and look for abstract meaning. Now remember, it is not a matter of either-or. Much good has come from the study of scripture and the intellectual tradition. Those in the past who chose to fight against such study accepted a fundamentalism that led to ignorance. What we need to do is recapture the wisdom of the intuitive way of thinking and knowing. We need to learn again to pray the scriptures.

Teaching and Preaching
to Engage the Imagination

One of the most insightful books written on teaching in the modern period is Maria Harris's *Teaching and the Religious Imagination.*[7] In it, she describes a way of teaching that speaks to our era and especially to the nurturing of the spiritual life. Her book also has important insights and implications for preaching and preparing to preach.

To provide a basis for her theory, Harris recounts a class taught by Mary Tully at Union Theological Seminary in New York. On this particular occasion, Tully gave each member of the class a piece of clay. She instructed the class to take a moment to be silent and clear their minds so that they could give their total attention to their clay. They were then to take time to make friends with their clay—to touch it, listen to it, smell it, taste it, and look at it. When they had become acquainted with their clay, they were to close their eyes and let the clay reveal to them what it would like to become. Once they were sure what the clay wanted to become, they were to open their eyes and assist the clay to actualize itself. Then, at a certain critical point, they were to cease their efforts and let it be.

This experience provided Harris with a framework for a model of teaching that engages the intuitive way of thinking and knowing.

The first movement is contemplation: a centering of ourselves, a standing back, a letting go, a being present, an opening of ourselves to the new.

The second movement is engagement: a relating to the other as a subject rather than an object, a process of becoming intimate with the other so that it might reveal something new and personal to us.

The third movement is form-giving: an engagement of our

creative imaginations in a process that makes possible a revelatory experience, out of which something new can emerge.

The fourth movement is emergence: a bringing to birth of the new; a naming of the learning, the insights and implications of our experience, in some concrete expression.

The last movement is release: a stopping, the putting of closure on our learning, so that we can begin the process again and increase our learning.

Imagine preaching a sermon or teaching a class following these movements. Imagine preaching and teaching that engage the religious imagination and lead both preachers and parishioners, teachers and students, into an experience of an ever-deepening and loving relationship to God. Imagine following these movements in the preparation of a sermon or a class. This is, I suggest, what we need to do if we are to take seriously a spiritual life for preaching and teaching.

It may be easier to imagine how this five-step process could be used in the creation of a sermon than how it could be applied to the delivery of a sermon, just as it may be easier to imagine the use of this model for teaching than its use for the development of a class session.

In preparing to teach, we need to free our minds of personal agendas and past experience, then permit our subject matter to engage us until it provides us with an insight into how it might engage others. The next step is to turn this insight into an implied process for a learning experience and then try it to see what occurs in the lives of those we have been called to teach.

In regard to a sermon, the process might look like this: First, provide for transition and silence before the reading of the Gospel so that persons may prepare themselves to hear it. Immediately after the reading, begin the sermon. Do so by taking others into the Gospel so that it might truly engage them as a subject. The next step is to provide an environment for persons to explore the Gospel's relevance and meaning for their lives. Once that possible meaning has emerged, take them to the Eucharist and reveal how it might provide them with the resource for making that new way of life possible. Such is the nature of the sermon in the context of the Eucharist: it begins with the Gospel, intersects with the community's life, and takes the community to the Holy Table and Communion.

3

The Spirituality of Preachers and Teachers

Alan Jones, in his book *Exploring Spiritual Direction,* provides us with an illuminating commentary on Graham Greene's novel *Dr. Fisher of Geneva, or the Bomb Party.* As Jones writes, the heroes of Greene's novels are often struggling in search of their own souls, or to put it in our words, to develop their spiritual lives.[1] In this particular novel, Greene describes the four requirements necessary for human beings to live in an ever-deepening and loving relationship to God.[2]

At one point, Greene's hero is talking with his wife about her malicious father, Dr. Fisher, and his strange friends. She asks, "Have you a soul?"

"I think I have one—shop worn but still there, but if souls exist you certainly have one."

"Why?"

"You've suffered."

One of Dr. Fisher's friends is Monsieur Belmont, a busy lawyer who specializes in tax evasion. As for a soul, "he hasn't time to develop one. . . . A soul requires a private life. Belmont has no time for a private life."

There is also a soldier, the Divisionaire, who "might possibly have a soul. There's something unhappy about him."

"And Mr. Kips?"

"I'm not sure about him either. There's a sense of disappointment about him. He might be looking for something he mislaid. Perhaps he's looking for his soul and not a dollar."

Then there is Richard Deane, the aging movie idol. "No, definitely not. No soul. I'm told he has copies of his old films and he plays them over every night to himself. . . . He's satisfied with himself. If you have a soul you can't be satisfied."

Last, there is Dr. Fisher himself, who unlike his hideous friends appears possibly to have satisfied these three requirements.

"And my father?" she asks.

"He has a soul all right, but I think it is a damned one."

There we have Graham Greene's four requirements for living a spiritual life: a willingness to embrace suffering, our own and the world's; a life marked by moments of silence and solitude; a willingness to pay attention to the deep restlessness in our spirits; and life within a community of faith that sees the image of God, the image of Christ, in us. The spirituality of preachers and teachers is dependent, I suggest, on a preacher or teacher meeting these four requirements or characteristics of life. Therefore, let us explore each of them.

Embracing Suffering

First is a willingness to embrace suffering, our own and the world's.

We are surely not to seek suffering or to wallow in it, but we are to acknowledge it and live in relationship to it. When we care for someone, we are willing to suffer with that person. To be able to have compassion for another implies that we have experienced suffering.

A story is told about a rabbi, a teacher, and one of his students. One day the student comes up to him and says, "Teacher, I love you."

"Do you know what hurts me?"

"No," says the young man, "I just wanted you to know I love you."

"But," the old man responds, "don't you understand? You cannot love me if you do not know what hurts me."

To preach or teach well requires a knowledge of that which hurts others. We need to know something of their pain, their sorrow, and their suffering. And we need to be aware of our own.

To care about people is not to desire to help them. When we have a desire to help people, then we go out of our way to keep them dependent on us, so we can be helpers. There are too many preachers and teachers who want to help people, to do something for them or to them. There need to be more preachers and teachers who desire only to be with others in ways that make it possible for them to help themselves. Christ did not fall into solution making or problem solving. That is our temptation. "Take my yoke," says Jesus. And what is his yoke? It is our suffering and the world's suffering. "My burden is light," he continues (see Matt. 11:29). It is light because he bears it with us.

Once I was presiding at an informal Eucharist for families. We had read a Gospel lesson about suffering, and I had asked if anyone knew anyone who was suffering. Several persons spoke, and then a young girl sitting next to her father said, "My father is suffering, but he will not tell anyone." And she hugged him.

Somewhat embarrassed, he said, "Jane, you're going to hug me to death."

"No," she explained, "I'm going to hug you to life."

A few days later, a mother told me a similar story. Her son was crippled, and she acknowledged that she had probably overprotected him, but one day she let him go to the store alone. When he did not return as rapidly as she thought he should, she hurried out to find out what happened. She found him limping up the street, whistling. "Where have you been?" she blurted out.

He responded, "I saw Carol, she dropped her doll and it broke."

"And you had to stay and help her pick it up," his mother continued.

"No, mother," he said, "I had to stay and help her cry."

The best teachers and preachers I have known are those who have embraced suffering. That is, they were persons who taught and preached out of the depths of their own life experience. We cannot live on the surface of life, avoiding or denying suffering, and still communicate the gospel. Good Friday is not the story of what evil people did to Jesus. Good Friday is the way God had established from the beginning to defeat evil. Easter is the "because" of Good Friday, not the "in spite of" it. Suffering and death are the way to new life.

It is those who know their need for forgiveness and who have experienced it who are able to communicate best through words and actions forgiveness to others. It is those who, from the depths of despair, have experienced God's redeeming power to transform despair into hope, sorrow into joy, and death into life who are able to communicate God's redemptive power in ways that make it possible for others to experience it. It is those who have been willing to be vulnerable and make themselves present to the sick, the homeless, the hungry, the poor, and the dying by embracing their suffering who are able to convince others of their calling to strive for justice and peace, no matter what the cost. It is those who have been able to identify with the weaknesses, the sin, the misery, and the needs of others, because they know their own, who are able to explain to others the nature of God's providence. To believe in providence is not to believe that everything turns out well or that everything is occurring according to a divine plan. Rather, faith in providence is an awareness that nothing and no one can prevent us from fulfilling the meaning and purpose of our lives, namely, to live in an ever-deepening and loving relationship to God.

Silence and Solitude

Second, we are to live lives marked by moments of silence and solitude. This is not easy in a world of noise and togetherness. Walker Percy, in his novel *The Second Coming,* has Will Barrett contemplating a lazy cat: "All at once he realized where he had gone wrong, there was the cat sitting in the sun one hundred percent cat and as for himself, Will had never been one hundred percent anything in his whole life."[3]

In my early days of teaching, I once began a class with from five to eight minutes of silence. After the second meeting of the class, a group of students came to see me. They were sure that I was wasting their time. They were paying a good deal to take this course, and we met only a few hours a week. They did not appreciate the silence. They wanted me to lecture. I asked, "Did you ever ponder the possibility that during the silence may be the only time you hear anything worth hearing this week?"

They had not. Sadly, they thought I was the one who was to teach them, not God's Spirit. Even sadder is the number of teachers and preachers I know who believe that they, not God's Spirit, are the teachers and preachers.

Such convictions are common. It is very difficult to maintain meaningful silence after the reading of scripture or after the sermon so that the Spirit might communicate with us.

Once, a student who enrolled in a course in which I required a weekend retreat came to say he could not go because he had responsibilities in a congregation on Sunday. I thought the issue was authority, so I said, "I'll write you an excuse."

"No," he exclaimed, "you don't understand, they need me."

"Why not leave a note on your door, 'Gone Praying'?" I quipped.

He didn't laugh. He just responded, "You don't understand. I'm needed."

In my last comment before he explained that he would have to drop the course, I added, "Maybe if you don't go on this retreat you will have nothing to bring them."

The problem is not limited to seminarians. There is a moving story told about Carl Jung, the psychiatrist, and one of his patients, a clergyman. Jung had suggested that his patient needed to take some time for silence and solitude each day. The clergyman, believing he was doing just that, set aside an hour each day, closed his study door, turned on soft music, and picked up a book to read. When he did not improve, he returned to see Jung. After he had explained what he was doing, Jung commented, "You have not been in silence and solitude. You have been spending your time with various musicians and authors. Why are you not willing to spend one hour each day with the self you inflict on others the rest of the day?"

There are too many people who believe that God created the world in six days and then took a day off to rest. Not so; the story is clear, it took God seven days to create the world. "And on the seventh day God finished the work that he had done" (Gen. 2:2). Sabbath, the seventh day, is part of creation, not a day added on.

People who live in the United States may be among the only English-speaking people in the world to use the word "vacation." They vacate or escape. Perhaps that is why they are often as tired when they return as when they left. The rest of the English-speaking world speaks of going on a holiday. One may feel guilty on a vacation; that is when one is "vacating," leaving behind one's responsibilities. But one never feels guilty on a holiday, a time made holy by God.

How often have you heard someone say, "I have never heard God say anything." Well, as noted earlier, if we treated people the way we treat God, people would not say anything either. Our greatest prayers are prayers of silence. What can we say? If we are honest, we really do not know what to pray for, so we listen. The foundational model for prayer in the New Testament is Jesus' in Gethsemane. It goes something like this: "God, what would you have me to do?" In the silence Jesus heard God affirming the call to suffer and die. Jesus, in response, said, "I'd just as soon not do that, but nevertheless your will be done"—and it is. When we pray, we are not to attempt to convince God to do what we would like. Rather, we are to give God permission to do what God desires to do. We know what the latter is only if we have been silent and heard the still, small voice of God informing us as to what to request.

Henri Nouwen somewhere commented that only in silence and solitude can we learn the important lessons that being is more important than having, that our worth is more than our efforts and not the same as our usefulness. Only when we can come to these conclusions can we communicate the gospel. There are too many teachers and preachers trying to make a difference rather than being willing to live in the difference that God has already made and continues to make, too many who want to be effective or successful when God has called them only to be faithful.

If we do not have a life marked by silence and solitude, we have nothing toward which to point a student and nothing worth rising into a pulpit to proclaim. Worse, in time our work will become drudgery rather than vocation.

Attention to Restlessness

Third, we need a willingness to pay attention to the deep restlessness in our lives. Unless we are growing, we have no right to try to help others grow. Unless we are in spiritual direction and have a developing spiritual life, we ought not offer others direction. If we are not learners, we ought not teach.

Indeed, unless we are growing in an ever-deepening and loving relationship to God, we cannot be faithful preachers or teachers.

Attending to our restlessness, of course, can be hard work, for it assumes continuous growth and change. It means living a life marked by critical reflection. It is easier to seek ways to escape, even in prayer. We humans are called to live lives of healthy dependence. We cannot be human alone. We are made to live in healthy relationships with one another. But that is difficult. Therefore, we need regularly to disengage from our human relationships and enter into a conscious state of total dependence on God. If we do this faithfully, God will engage us and transform our lives and then send us back into the world as spiritually healthier persons. Regretfully, however, people often come to prayer to escape life and its problems rather than to be engaged and changed. When they seek escape, they may return rested but never more healthy. To benefit from prayer, we need to prepare. We need to take the time to reflect on our lives and listen to where God's Spirit is calling us. We then need to permit God to engage us, anticipating that God will empower us to follow that calling.

The spiritual life is a pilgrimage. It is not a pilgrimage, however, to become something we are not, a work of our own doing. It is rather a process of becoming who we already are, that is, who by God's grace we have been made and who through God's grace we will be enabled to become. It is similar to our baptism, a reality into which we are always living, becoming who we already are.

To show how listening to our spirits is an integral part of that life, Ignatius of Loyola suggests two exercises: the examination of consciousness and the examination of conscience. In the first, we review our day to remember a moment when we experienced God's presence and action in our lives. Then, in our imaginations, we experience that grace again. Having done so, we go back to the other moments in our day where we were unaware of God's presence and action. With sorrow for our lack of consciousness, we ask God to reveal to us where God was present and active. Then we give thanks for that new awareness and ask God to reveal to us what grace we need and God desires to give us, so that we might be increasingly more conscious of God's presence and action in the future. Last, we ask for that grace, knowing that God has already willed to give it to us.

The examination of conscience begins by our going back to a moment in our lives when we experienced God's grace, God's redeeming presence and action, and in our imaginations bathing in that grace again. Having done that, we are to become aware of where we have recently experienced brokenness and incompleteness. We are then to ask God to heal us, and we are to open ourselves to God's transforming healing power. Next, we ask God to reveal to us to what new behaviors we are being called in the light of God's healing. Last, we are to give ourselves, in our imagination, to the practice of this new behavior. So it is that we learn to move from grace to grace in our lives.

If we are to preach and teach, we need to make sure that we are paying attention to the restlessness of our spirits and that we are growing in an ever-deepening and loving relationship to God and therefore to our true, healthy selves, to all those to whom we preach or teach, and to all of God's creation.

Image of Christ

Last, we all need to live in a community that sees in us the image of God, the image of Christ. To preach and to teach are to offer an example of that which is possible and necessary for all people. We are all to seek and serve Christ in all persons, loving our neighbor as God loves us. Sin is the denial and distortion of the truth. The truth about each and every human being is that he or she is in the image of God. At one time or another, all of us deny or distort that image. What we all require is life in a community that sees in us that image and treats us accordingly, thereby helping us to become aware of our sin, to repent, and to live out the truth about ourselves. We cannot do that for others unless others are doing that for us. Faithful preaching and teaching require an awareness of how much in need we are of life in a community of faith. We are as dependent on the community as it is on us.

An old teaching suggests that when we walk down the street, we are to imagine that there is a host of angels in front of us, in everyone we meet. They are all crying, "Make way for the image of God! Make way for the image of God!" Charles Williams, the English author, is said to have commented that if everyone could perceive that reality, everyone would walk with head held high and fall in love with everyone he or she meets.

Catharine Dougherty, the spiritual writer, tells a beautiful story about her friend Dorothy Day. One night, when the snow was falling, there was a knock on the door of their tenement in New York. At the door was a woman looking for a place to stay. Dorothy Day commented, "Oh my, we are already full, but come in, you can sleep with me."

Dougherty is said to have taken her aside and asked, "Don't you see that woman is in the last stages of syphilis?"

"No," her friend is said to have responded, "I can see only the image of Christ." To teach or preach, we need to live in a community that sees that image in us so that we might reveal it to others.

Last Thoughts

Teachers and preachers require spiritual lives that embrace suffering and that are in touch with the depths of existence;

lives that are marked by moments of silence and solitude, lived in a rhythm between contemplation and action; lives that are self-critical, that pay attention to the deep restlessness of our spirits, and respond to God's call to grow spiritually; and lives that are lived in a community of faith comprised of persons who see the image of God in us even when we deny and distort it.

4

The Spirituality of Preaching and Teaching

Henri Nouwen once recounted a Buddhist tale that went something like this: Once upon a time, there was a young man in search of goodness, truth, and beauty. After many years of failure, he came upon an old holy man and asked him to be his teacher. The old man said that of course he would be his teacher and then made the young man his servant. For three years the young man followed the old man about, cooked his meals, washed his clothes, carried his supplies, and the like, but the old man said not a word to him. At last, in frustration and desperation, the young man cried out, "I gave up everything to follow you and you have taught me nothing."

The old man responded, "But my son, haven't you been with me all these years?"

At that point the young man was enlightened.

Nouwen commented that within this tale were the three foundational truths of all profound spiritual teaching and learning: someone must be searching; someone must be willing to let her or his life be a resource for the other's learning; and if there is any truth, it will break in from the outside and illumine both the teacher and the learner. The spirituality of teaching and preaching is to be found in those three insights. Let us, therefore, explore them one at a time.

Someone Searching

First, there is no true learning if someone is not searching. How often do we engage in teaching and preaching with the conviction that there is something that someone else needs to know? We go about our task faithfully, but we have unsatisfactory results. Few, if any, learn what someone else wants them to know, care about, or do. It is somewhat like my reaction to those who come to me and say, "You need to know, . . . ," to which I have typically responded, "No, you are wrong. I do not need to know. You apparently need to tell me."

No one can force another to learn. We can, through one or another positive or negative manipulative means, get someone to repeat what we say or do what we did, that is, pass a test. But that does not mean that the other learned it. The lowest level of knowledge is repeating back what someone has said. Comprehension follows, but that requires that someone can put what one has heard into one's own words. Only then can anyone use what has been heard for some purpose. Having learned to apply what one has heard to some task, one is then ready to analyze what was heard, that is, to discover how that position was reached and compare and contrast it with other positions. Only then is it possible for someone to develop one's own position based on available information. Then comes the highest form of knowledge, the ability to make a judgment on a particular proposition's or conclusion's truth or value. Most people never learn to do that, because that ability is dependent on mastering all the other levels of knowledge. Instead, believing that they are making value judgments, they offer only uninformed, passionate opinions that have little value and cannot be argued or reconciled.

In any case, without questions, answers are oppressive manipulations. However, when someone has a question, then that person wants to learn and will learn, indeed, and will always remember what has been learned.

The most difficult thing for a preacher or teacher to do is to be willing to wait patiently for a question, that is, to neither resist nor run until the learner is ready. We need to listen carefully for the questions being asked and then encourage and stimulate other questions. Preaching and teaching are, first of all, creating the space for the developing of questions and the search for answers. Every child is a searcher, a natural searcher. Regrettably, over time children learn not to search, because adults are too busy showing them where to look. They learn not to ask questions, because adults are busy providing them with the answers. Then, as they get older, preachers and teachers continue to tell them what the preachers and teachers believe they need to know, only now, as adults, they just passively listen and typically ignore what is offered.

True preaching and teaching require a spiritual posture of giving up control and floating. When we swim, we always pit our will against the water, and the water eventually wins. But if we float, we survive. Floating is not passively doing nothing. It is an action of cooperating with the water. While floating is natural for human beings, it is one of the most difficult things to learn because we want so badly to be in control.

Perhaps our most foundational or original sin is the desire to be in control and the conviction that we can and should be in control. To that extent, we all manifest addictive behavior. Workaholics may be more numerous than alcoholics, but they are no healthier. As all twelve-step programs recognize, the first step toward health is an acknowledgment that we are not and can never be in control, followed by an acknowledgment that there is a power to which we can turn for help. Then comes the big move. We must turn our trust over to that power.

The Episcopal Church's baptismal rite calls on people to do just that. After baptismal candidates have renounced evil, they do three things: first, they acknowledge Jesus as their Savior, that is, they confess that their lives are out of their control and that only dependence on Jesus can free them for new and responsible lives; second, they put their whole trust in his grace and love; and third, they promise to follow and obey him. From then on, they, along with all the baptized, are recovering addicts, redeemed sinners. As preachers and teachers, we need to give up our desire to be in control and to control. We need to be willing simply to be present to others in ways that make them aware of their questions and quest. The spirituality of teaching reminds us of the importance of the pilgrims' search, and the teachers and preachers need to give up control and wait for the searchers' quest.

Of course, preachers and teachers need to be searchers themselves if they want to encourage others to search. They need to model question-asking if they expect others to do the same. There is nothing wrong with not having answers. Preachers and teachers are at their best when they can say, "I do not know, but I will not leave you alone with your question. I will search with you for an answer."

Lives as a Source for Learning

Second, once preachers or teachers are aware of the questions, they need to realize that their lives are to be the resource for the searchers' learning. A Taoist tale powerfully illumines this truth: Once a man entered the land of fools. He saw everyone running from a field screaming, "There's a monster in the field!"

When he looked, he saw that their monster was a watermelon. He said to himself, "I'll teach these stupid people the difference between monsters and watermelon."

So he went into the field, picked up the watermelon, cut a piece out of it, and ate it. The people watched in astonishment.

Then they ran to kill him shouting, "He's killed the monster and will kill us."

A few years later, another man entered the land of the fools and encountered a similar situation, only in this case he ran with them and lived among them. Aware that their monster was a watermelon, he slowly and gradually encouraged them to watch closely, and slowly he moved closer to it, thereby demonstrating that it was safe. Then one day the people discovered that the monster was really a fruit to eat and enjoy. Who, asks the Taoist, was the true teacher? The answer is, the one who let his life be a resource for the others' learning.

It has always been true. Benjamin Jacobs, the Baptist layman who helped to transform the Sunday school into a worldwide movement, spoke of teaching as leading others by example on the road to spiritual maturity. "Children," he pointed out, "may never study their Bibles as diligently as desired, but they will always study the lives of the adults they meet in the church. Teachers, therefore, must be models of what they desire others to become."[1]

A few years later, L. F. Senabaugh wrote, "Surely not just anyone can teach, for religion is caught more than taught and we can not teach what we do not know and have not verified. A teacher may teach about Christianity, but if the teacher is to teach Christ, he must live in fellowship with him."[2] The same can and needs to be said about preachers.

Alice Walker, in her book *Revolutionary Petunias and Other Poems*, has a poem titled "Sunday School, Circa 1950":

> "Who made you?" was always
> The question
> The answer was always
> "God."
> Well, there we stood
> Three feet high

Heads bowed
Leaning into
Bosoms.

Now
I no longer recall
The Catechism
Or brood on the Genesis
Of life
No.

I ponder the exchange
Itself
And salvage mostly
The leaning.[3]

I will never forget observing the behavior of a preschool teacher many years ago. The teacher was moving from free time to group time by encouraging the children to put away their toys. When she got to Johnny, she asked, "Johnny, will you help me put your blocks away?"

Johnny looked up and said, "No."

Without skipping a beat, the teacher went on, "Well, today I'll help you and perhaps tomorrow you will help me."

Having put the blocks away, she turned. Johnny, who had been watching, picked up a block and threw it at her, striking her in the head. The teacher turned around and drew Johnny into her arms, saying, "Johnny, I suspect you are angry at me, and I'm angry with you, but we both have to learn to talk with our mouths and not with our hands; and anyway, I need to hold you until I feel better about myself."

In a few moments, he stopped kicking and screaming. She let him go and while she turned to the group, he went off to play with the blocks once again. However, in a very short time, he left the blocks, made his way over to the group, sat in her lap, interrupted the story, and said, "I like you."

That is the experience of reconciliation. Someday, when Johnny gets around to asking what reconciliation means and someone gives him a definition, he will truly know what it means and be enabled to act that way himself. The reason is that this teacher was able to let her life be a resource for his learning.

Another way of explaining it is to say that we are called to preach and teach the way Jesus did. In Jesus' day, rabbis traditionally made their home in a synagogue. Students would come to them and say, Please be my teacher. If the rabbi agreed, they would sit at the rabbi's feet and take notes on what he said. It is the schooling model of teaching that we all know so well. But Jesus was different. He went out in search of students—those who were searching—and told them to identify with him, to come live with him, to observe how he behaved and imitate him. It was an apprenticeship model of preaching and teaching, in which the preacher-teacher let his life be a resource for the students' learning.

This pattern of instruction perhaps will help us understand why the early church titled the second half of Luke's writing the Acts of the Apostles and not the talk of the apostles. It also should help us understand why James, the brother of Jesus and the first bishop of Jerusalem, in what tradition says was a sermon delivered to catechumens preparing for baptism, comments, "Not many of you should become teachers, my brothers and sisters, for you know that we who teach will be judged with greater strictness" (James 3:1).

There are three possible metaphors for curriculum or the course that we humans are called on to run. The first is an assembly line. Children and other learners are valuable pieces of raw material. Teachers and preachers are skilled technicians because they have studied teaching and preaching. The process is one of molding each valuable piece of raw material into the teacher's or preacher's predetermined design.

Teachers and preachers do things to people. Have we not all known teachers and preachers who have behaved in this manner? Our quest, our search, does not matter. Their lives are never a resource for our learning. They know what we need to believe and how we are to behave. "Do as I say and not necessarily as I do" is their motto. I know what is best for you. Just relax and let me mold you as I see fit.

A second metaphor is a greenhouse. Now the child or learner is a seed. The teacher or preacher is a gardener. The process is caring for each seed until it grows up to be what is intended. Of course, the gardener is knowledgeable in what the seed is to become; how the seed grows; and how much sun, water, and fertilizer it requires. In this case, the teacher or preacher does not do things to the learner; the teacher or preacher does things for the learner. Once again, the life of the teacher or preacher is not intended to be a resource for learning. Through their studies, the teacher and preacher know what nurture and nourishment is needed for the seed to grow, and their role is to help the seed grow accordingly. I want to help you. Let me take care of you. Be dependent on me for your well-being, they explain.

The third metaphor is that of a pilgrimage. Now the child or learner is a pilgrim. The teacher or preacher is a co-pilgrim. The process is a shared journey over time. Now the teacher or preacher does things with the learner. Both are on a quest, each is searching. Each, at one time or another, is letting the other be a resource for learning. There is a mutuality of living together on a common quest that binds them into community and permits God's Spirit to influence their learning and growth.

We often forget that the word "authority" means the right to be heard, not to be believed or obeyed. There are many possible reasons for granting someone authority. There is structural authority, the right to be heard by the nature of one's office, in this case, as teacher or preacher. This form of authority has the least legitimacy.

There is also "sapiential" authority, the right to be heard by reason of one's proven wisdom; personal authority, the right to be heard by reason of one's being or personhood; moral authority, the right to be heard by reason of one's character; and charismatic authority, the right to be heard by the action of God's spirit in one's life. All of these forms of authority are important for teachers and preachers.

Behind these understandings of authority is another, more foundational understanding, namely, the source for knowing how we are to live. For Christians, this authority is the triune God, a God whose way we come to know through the foundational authority of the Holy Scriptures and the interpretative authorities of reason and tradition. It is the Holy Spirit who leads us into all truth and enables us to grow in the life of Christ. Indeed, we understand the scriptures only by the help of the Holy Spirit, who guides the church in their true interpretation.

One of the major problems for preachers and teachers is that they have been schooled in a way of knowing that treats people and the world as objects for their study and manipulation. Parker Palmer, in his seminal work *To Know As We Are Known,* makes the same point.[4] Preachers and teachers have relied on the social sciences to explain personal and social behavior and to provide them with insights on how to influence others. We need to acknowledge that people and, indeed, the whole of creation are not objects for us to engage but subjects that engage us. People are always best understood as mysteries and surprises.

Preachers and teachers are moral agents. They have the potential of influencing people and therefore should be very careful in what they say and do. Preachers and teachers are political agents. They are part of a community of the faith and have an obligation to that community and its traditions. And preachers and teachers are artistic agents. They arrange environments for learning.

Truth Breaks In

Third, we need to acknowledge and be open to that truth that always breaks in from a source beyond both the preacher or teacher and the learner.

I heard Henri Nouwen once tell this story: He was sitting in his office when a student came to see him. The student said, "I have nothing to ask you or say to you. I just wanted to be silent with you."

After they sat in silence for a while, the student said, "Whenever I'm in your presence, it is as if I am in the presence of Christ."

Nouwen responded, "It is the Christ in you that sees the Christ in me."

The student said, "From now on, wherever I go, all the ground between us will be holy ground."

Commented Nouwen, "At that point it was revealed to both of us what community meant."

For me, this great insight on the spirituality of preaching and teaching became a reality at a conference center outside Belfast, where I had been invited to lead a conference on baptism for Roman Catholic and Protestant clergy. At the same time there was a group of children from these two communions gathered to get to know each other better and thereby reduce the prejudice and hostility toward each other. Each morning I was to begin with simple prayers acceptable to both Roman Catholics and Protestants. Each day I told a Bible story about healing and reconciliation, and we sat in silence. The two groups had spent much of the week arguing with each other and talking past each other. I felt like a failure as a teacher. Then one morning a Roman Catholic monk chose to break the pattern of adults sitting in chairs while the children sat on the floor. He chose to sit with the children. That morning, in the mystery of things, I had chosen to tell the story of the woman who touched the hem of Jesus' cloak and was healed. In the silence that followed, whispers could be heard between a little Protestant girl and the Roman Catholic monk.

"Can I touch you?" she asked.

"Of course," he said.

"I'm scared."

"Why?"

"If my father knew I touched you, he might beat me."

"Perhaps he does not need to know." Then she reached out a finger and touched him. Looking at her finger she exclaimed, "Nothing happened!"

With tears welling up in his eyes, the monk said, "Yes, it did. You and I will never see the world the same again."

After that morning, everything changed in the conversations between those who had gathered in the name of reconciliation.

There we have it. The spirituality of preaching and teaching requires that someone is searching, someone is willing to let his or her life be a resource for the searcher's learning, and both are open to that truth which breaks in on them from a source outside themselves, through the action of God's Spirit.

5

Various Ways of Living Spiritually

The spiritual life is concerned with our relationship with God. Prayer is both any means that aids this relationship and the manifestation of this relationship. The first is prayer as devotional activity, and the second is prayer as daily life. In this chapter we are concerned with prayer as devotional activity, as spiritual exercise.

Urban Holmes presents a helpful typology for the spiritual life in his insightful book *A History of Spirituality*.[1] He suggests that there have always been two appropriate ends for the spiritual life: a speculative spirituality that focuses on the illumination of the mind and an affective spirituality that focuses on the illumination of the heart. He further suggests there are two appropriate means toward those ends: a kataphatic means, an indirect way of knowing in which our relationship with God is mediated, and an apophatic means, a direct way of knowing, in which our relationship with God is not mediated.

Schools of Spirituality

The resulting typology contains four schools of spirituality: speculative-kataphatic, affective-kataphatic, affective-apophatic, and speculative-apophatic (see figure 1). Each of these schools is subject to a natural heresy. A heresy is a truth

---

53

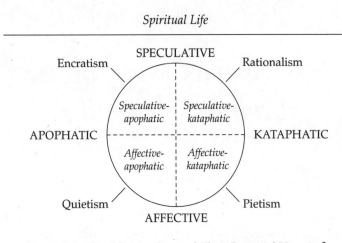

Fig. 1. Schools of Spirituality and Their Potential Heresies[2]

that has gone too far, that has denied its countertruth. For example, the speculative-kataphatic school, if it denies the validity of the affective-apophatic school, will fall into the heresy of rationalism, an excessive concern for right thinking that leads to dogmatism. The affective-kataphatic school risks falling into the heresy of pietism, an excessive concern for right feelings that leads to emotionalism. The affective-apophatic school is subject to the heresy of quietism, an excessive concern for right interior experience that leads to escapism; and the speculative-apophatic school may fall into the heresy of encratism, an excessive concern for right behavior that leads to moralism. Each school, then, needs to be held in tension with its opposite. Now let us look at each one of these schools.

Speculative-kataphatic

The speculative-kataphatic school can be identified as sacramental. Its primary aim is to aid persons in fulfilling their vocation in the world. Its major concerns are the discernment of God's will, the discernment of spirits, the imitation of Jesus, and becoming aware of God's presence and action in human life and history. It is a thinking spirituality and includes historic persons such as Ignatius of Loyola, Martin Luther, Augustine, and Dag Hammarskjöld.

This school is dominated by mental prayer or meditation, a process of engaging the senses in reflecting on or musing over an experience of a painting, a poem, a piece of music, or the scriptures. The rosary is a mental prayer that combines familiar, repetitive prayers with meditations on the joyful, sorrowful, and glorious mysteries of the Christian faith (the incarnation, crucifixion, and resurrection and ascension), which are able to communicate depths of spiritual meaning beyond the obvious.

Meditative prayers for dealing with disordered affections are another example of this kind of prayer. In prayers for disordered affections, if, for example, we are angry, we take the person we are angry with before God and in our imaginations speak and act out our anger until we can do so no longer. Then we are to be silent so that God can fill the open space we have created in our minds with God's love.

Another expression of prayers consists of writing out conversations with God, as are often found in spiritual journals. In any case, all expressions of prayer in this school make use of the imagination, the senses, and the intellect, which are intended to help persons acquire insights and implications for their lives by being attentive to God's Spirit.

Affective-kataphatic

The affective-kataphatic school can be identified as charismatic. Its primary aim is to achieve holiness of life. Its major concerns are friendship with Jesus, an outpouring of the Spirit, and providing a sign of God's reign through personal and communal life. It is a sensate, feeling spirituality and includes historic persons such as Benedict of Nursia, Julian of Norwich, John Wesley, George Herbert, and Martin Luther King, Jr. It might be helpful to point out here that persons within any school of spirituality will likely manifest characteristics from their counterschool, in this case the speculative-apophatic school. If they do so, they prevent themselves from falling into their school's natural heresy.

This school is dominated by verbal-sensate prayer. Here the whole body, all of the senses—speaking, tasting, touching, smelling, and listening—and the emotions, is involved. It can take the form of beautiful vocal prayers, whether they are contained in prayer books, written originally, or spoken spontaneously. This type of praying begins with adoration (I love you, God) and continues with praise (you are ever-forgiving), thanksgiving (I am grateful for . . .), oblation (I give my life to you), contrition (I am sorry for . . .), intercession (please do . . . for . . .), and last, petition (I desire . . .). It can take the form of chanting the Psalms or singing gospel hymns.

Another example from this school is the devotion known as the Way of the Cross. In this devotion persons, alone or with others, walk the trying, painful Via Dolorosa with Jesus, singing and stopping along the way at fourteen stations to listen to the scriptures and pray, so as to experience and emotionally identify with Jesus' actions on our behalf in order that we might learn to follow in the way of the cross.

Prayer that involves clapping, touching, body movement, shouting, and the free expression of emotion is typical of the affective-kataphatic school. Different racial and ethnic groups have different cultural manifestations of these devotional activities and may appear radically different. For example, an African-American gospel hymn sung with spontaneous prayers and an Anglo-Catholic evensong with ancient written prayers both emerge from the same school of spirituality.

Affective-apophatic

The affective-apophatic school is mystical. Its primary aim is to be united with God. Its major concerns are pointing to the reality of God's reign and abiding in that reality. It is a spirituality that emphasizes being and includes historic persons such as Teresa of Avila, John of the Cross, Thomas Münzer, Thomas Merton, Howard Thurman, George Fox, and most of Eastern Orthodox spirituality.

This school is dominated by contemplative prayer. Centering prayers are typical. Their purpose is to occupy and free the mind so that one may dwell with God. The rattling off of prayers known by heart can achieve the same purpose. The oldest prayers in the church are centering prayers such as "Lord Jesus Christ, Son of God, have mercy on me, a sinner." Listening to Eastern music that has no set rhythm or story line; fantasy exercises; gazing on an icon; or participation in a devotion such as the Benediction of the Blessed Sacrament after evening prayer, a solemn adoration of the crucified and risen Christ present among us in the form of a consecrated Host within a monstrance, are forms of prayer in this school.

Often people are confused about this school because it includes both the Quakers and the Eastern Orthodox. What we need to remember is that both have the same end, the emptying of the self from all distractions so as to be fully aware of the Holy Spirit and its activity within our lives. The first group does this by creating empty, white space where there is nothing to stimulate the senses and silence rules. The other makes use of the senses as a means of eliminating their influence. For example, Western painting, music, and incense are intended to stimulate our senses, but within the Eastern Orthodox Church, the icon, music, and incense are intended to do the opposite. One gazes on an icon to be taken through it, so as to make direct contact with the mystery that is spiritually present but hidden.

Speculative-apophatic

The speculative-apophatic school can be identified as apostolic. Its primary aim is to obey God's will completely. Its major concerns are witness to God's reign and striving for justice and peace. It is a spirituality that emphasizes spirituality and includes historic persons such as Dominic, John Calvin, Catherine of Genoa, and Dorothy Day.

This school is dominated by active prayer. For many, this is the most difficult to understand. Spiritual reading, listening to quiet day homilies, taking a hike, playing music, drawing, and dancing in silence are forms of active prayer. So are fasting, the giving of alms, and the performance of acts of mercy. While for most people such acts are a response to devotional prayer, for those in this school, they are the prayer itself. For example, one might have a friend who is having a problem with alcohol. A responsible prayer for someone in this school of spirituality would be for the person who is praying to stop drinking alcoholic beverages but not to tell the alcoholic friend of his or her concern, because that would be manipulation and not prayer. The prayer is one's own action on a friend's behalf.

One devotion from this school concerns a way to pray the Lord's Prayer based on the understanding that each phrase is intended to be a question that we are to bring to God each day. Thus we can be aware of how God would like us to behave and, having responded appropriately, receive the power to do so. The following questions, for example, are derived from the Lord's Prayer and prompt emulation:

"What do you want to make holy and whole in my life this day?"

"How can your reign come through me this day?"

"For what do I need to be forgiven, and with whom do I need to be reconciled?"

Personality and Prayer

Each of these schools of spirituality provides us with different ways to pray. The test of these prayers is always the same: Do they enhance and enliven a person's relationship to God? Most people find that one way of prayer is more to their liking and aids them more than another in their relationship with God. One of the factors that appears to affect our preference is our personality. The work of Carl Jung on personality theory, especially as it has been interpreted by Isabel Briggs-Myers through her personality inventory and by David Kersey and Marilyn Bates through their temperament sorter, has provided the theoretical base for this contention.

To simplify this particular personality theory for the purposes of this chapter, consider four characteristics that Jung suggests comprise the human personality. The first has to do with how a person acquires and dispenses energy. Those who acquire energy by being alone and expend it on people Jung calls "introverts." Those who acquire energy from people and expend it while being alone he calls "extroverts." Introversion (I) and extroversion (E) have nothing to do with being shy or liking people. They have to do with how our batteries are charged, not our particular social skills. Indeed, many very public people such as actors and actresses are introverts. Their public activity, as enjoyable as it is, drains them, and therefore after a performance they need to get away and be alone. Introverts tend to find personal prayer more to their liking and extroverts turn to communal prayer. Introverts go on a retreat to acquire energy while extroverts go on a retreat to expend it. Those planning retreats need to take these differing needs seriously.

The second characteristic of the human personality is concerned with how people gather data from the world. Those whom Jung calls "sensate" people (S) gather their data through their senses, that is, through what they can see, touch, taste, feel, and smell. The others he calls "intuitive" (N). They gather their data through their imaginations. For example, I am an extreme "N." I have always questioned anything that can be seen, touched, tasted, smelled, heard, but I have a vivid imagination, which I find more trustworthy. In my first parish, I made a theological statement that I believed was faithful and orthodox: "I do not care if they find Jesus' bones, I believe in the resurrection; I do not care if they prove that Mary was impregnated with Joseph's sperm, I believe in the virgin birth." Those truths were and always have been for me in the mystery of the human imagination, but for my congregation of mostly sensate people, my statements were apostasy. They could believe in these affirmations of faith only if they could be sensually established.

Third, Jung differentiates between those who process their data from the world through rational thinking processes and those who process through what is best described as an internal sense of rightness. Thinking types (T) are no more intellectual than feeling types (F); nor are thinking types brighter or lacking in feeling. Likewise, feeling types are not necessarily more caring or comfortable with their feeling. These categories best describe two ways of thinking and knowing: in thinking types the intellect is dominant, and in feeling types the intuition is dominant.

The fourth characteristic of the human personality identified by Jung has to do with whether people feel the need for high structure and closure or a need for low structure and lack of closure. The first he called "judgmental" (J) and the second "perceptive" (P). As ought to be obvious, the first tend to find structured, formal prayer more meaningful, whereas the latter prefer spontaneous, informal prayer. As a strong "J," I have never been comfortable with informal prayers.

Now, if a person is rated in terms of each of these characteristics, the result is a particular personality type, such as my own "INTJ." Each characteristic, however, is solely a matter of preferred dominance. Therefore, persons who share the same characteristics may, in fact, be quite different. For example, I am at the extreme on the first two (I and N), on the third my "T" and "F" are close but the "T" clearly dominates, and on the fourth I am definitely a strong "J" with only a little "P."

Further, all of us can learn to use the other functions. Indeed, at particular times in our lives, our experience may cause a change in a dominant characteristic, especially if our preference for one or the other is not at the extreme. These types, like the schools of spirituality, are not boxes into which we can put people. They are simply typologies that can be helpful to us in understanding ourselves and others, especially those who are different from us.

Many books are available that identify these categories with the four schools of spirituality.[3] Typically, they place "ST's" in the speculative-kataphatic school, the "SF's" in the affective-kataphatic, the "NF's" in the affective-apophatic, and the "NT's" in the speculative-apophatic. These identifications in my experience have never proven to be helpful. Having struggled with this problem for some time, I returned to Jung and discovered his contention that only the stronger of the two middle traits is a useful indicator of behavior. For example, in my case, as an "INTJ," my dominant middle trait is the "N."

Therefore, according to this insight, there are four categories available: T, S, N, and F. The schools of spirituality and personality types look like this: speculative-apophatic = T; speculative-kataphatic = S; affective-apophatic = N; affective-kataphatic = F (see figure 2). This corresponds to my experience and makes sense in terms of having the schools of prayer correspond to various personality preferences.

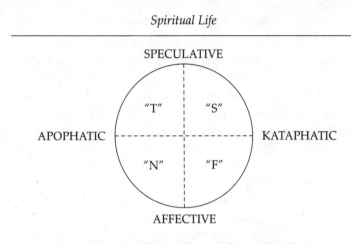

SPECULATIVE

"T"   "S"

APOPHATIC —————————————— KATAPHATIC

"N"   "F"

AFFECTIVE

Fig. 2. Schools of Spirituality and Personality Types

There is one other insight that Jung offers. He suggests that we need to differentiate in our lives between work and leisure; I would say, between daily life and devotional prayer. Jung contends that if our personality needs are met in our life of work, we will seek their very opposite in our leisure. I have found it to be true that if our personality needs are met in our daily lives, then we will find devotional prayer in our counter-school of spirituality more satisfying. However, if our world of work does not meet our personality needs, we will seek to have them met through our devotional prayer life. So it is that I move back and forth between mystical-contemplative prayer and sacramental-mental prayer. Apostolic-active prayer and charismatic-sensate prayer only rarely serve my needs.

Last Thoughts

There are important implications from these insights. There are many ways to pray. No one way is useful for all persons. Wholeness is best understood in communal rather than personal terms. Each person does not need to incorporate all of the various ways of prayer, but we do need a sense of community large enough to include all of the various means. Religious orders and denominations may have a dominant personality and represent a particular school of spirituality, but we need to affirm and support others who are different, for they represent a piece of the whole. What we will discover is that if there are vast differences within a community, we may have difficulty serving everyone's needs.

Often persons representing opposite schools of spirituality, though they need each other to avoid falling into their own school's heresy, experience conflict with each other because they are so different. Those who represent schools of spirituality different from but somewhat similar to our own are often the most difficult to comprehend.

To summarize, prayer is any means (it can never be an end in itself) that aids us in our relationship with God (the end and aim of all human life). There are many ways to pray, and each is tested by how well it aids us in our spiritual growth. In that regard, let us remember that there is a theology and a morality to prayer. If our prayers are aiding us to grow in relationship to a god—an ultimate reality—such as economic success, which is not God, then our praying cannot be theologically justified. Further, our praying needs to be moral. If, for example, a person hears a fire truck coming down the street and prays, "God, may it not be my house," that person is uttering an immoral prayer because he or she is willing it to be someone else's house. It would be better to pray, "God, may it be my house, but may no one be hurt." Of course, in our humanness we might cry out the first prayer, but we ought not to believe that God will answer it. If, then, we return home and find the house safe, there is no reason to thank God. To relate to a God who created the world but is no longer present and active makes little sense. But neither does it make sense to pray to a God who has a preconceived plan that will evolve in spite of us, or to a God who is present and active doing things to us or for us against our will. To pray faithfully is to be continually engaged in critical reflection on our praying in the light of the gospel, so that we might continually reform, enhance, and enliven our prayer life as necessary.

6

Developing a Spiritual Discipline

A discipline is something we practice, an exercise. While in this case we are discussing ways to develop a discipline that will aid us in developing our spiritual lives, our relationship with God, the best metaphors that I know of for this come from the disciplines related to physical health. For me, this means, among other things, jogging. Just as when I think about a metaphor for my spiritual life I turn to friendship, when I think of a spiritual discipline I turn to jogging.

For example, when I began to jog, I needed to find the right time of day. I discovered that for me it was the first thing in the morning. The afternoon or evening just did not work, although they did for many of my friends. In the beginning, my discipline was a forced routine of walking first and then slowly jogging over the same route. On many days I had to force myself to do it; now it comes naturally, and if for some reason I neglect it, I miss it. The first thing I learned was the necessity of preparation, of stretching out. If I did not do that or hurried the preparation, the run did not go as well. In the beginning, I only walked a short distance. Little by little, I built up the time and speed. If I did too much too soon, I paid a price. When I neglected the daily exercise, I discovered I could not pick up where I had left off. I had to go back and begin again as if I had not advanced very far. I also learned that when I was finished, I had to stretch out and relax before

I took my shower. Now the routine is very natural, four miles, thirty minutes (five minutes warm-up at the beginning and sweat-down at the end). Each day I feel better if I jog, even though I often do not desire to do so or have commitments that prevent me from doing so. I have learned that I must be disciplined and participate in my physical discipline no matter what, and I have also learned that if I do, I feel better.

When I was on leave from Duke and serving as interim rector of a parish, I discovered how difficult it is to find time to read those scholarly books that at the moment appear to have no practical relevance. In the academy I had a great deal of time to do that sort of reading. While on leave, I realized that if my mind was to be as disciplined as my spirit and body, I had to develop a mental discipline. I therefore added an hour of such reading each day, and it felt good. Each day I now spend an hour in prayer, an hour in exercise, and an hour reading scholarly books. These three hours are foundational to my life as teacher and preacher, but at the center of the three is my spiritual discipline. To keep my metaphor of physical exercise going, every coach has her or his way of helping her or his players to develop a physical discipline. Yet a self-discipline is superior to one imposed by another person. Eventually, each and every one of us needs to develop our own discipline. Therefore, please take what follows only as suggestions.

Time and Place

Review a typical day. There will be moments when your mind typically is racing and times when you could easily fall into sleep. There will be times when you are always hungry or in need of exercise. What you need to do is identify those middle times when other needs are least pressing. Then review your week in terms of those middle times and pick one in which you are least apt to be distracted or have demands made on you. Remember, you can always leave a message on your answering machine that you are at prayer from eight to nine and will return the call later.

Next, begin with a small amount of time, perhaps once a week for five minutes, for example. Build up slowly until you reach your goal. At the end of the first year, thirty minutes, four days a week might be reasonable. Find a place in which you can experience silence and solitude. Some can do that while riding on a crowded bus, but others require a chapel. I do not recommend trying to pray while at the wheel of your car, because if you succeed in achieving the desired intimacy with God, you will become a danger on the highway. It is not that you cannot be aware of God's presence and have some sort of relationship with God while driving. You can—just as you can, for example, enjoy your relationship with your husband or wife while driving. But driving a car is no time for intimate lovemaking—an activity important to a healthy marriage.

Some people need a plain room without any distractions, and others need a room filled with sensual stimulation and religious symbols. Just as, in the beginning, you need to be rigid in following your discipline, you need to maintain a regular time and familiar space. Later, you can change your times and move to different spaces.

Preparation

The first step is to clear your mind and heart so that you can focus your full attention on God. There is no one way to do this. An exercise I sometimes use is to imagine lying peacefully on the bottom of a pond watching bubbles coming out of my mouth, floating up to the surface, and then disappearing. I imagine that the bubbles are carrying the thoughts and concerns, emotions and feelings I am experiencing at the moment. Some people have discovered that writing lists, especially of things to do, helps.

Next, it is important to relax your body. I sometimes do the same stretching exercises I do before jogging and then sit down and relax by taking some very deep breaths. My favorite exercise, however, is to pray a centering prayer. A centering prayer is a word or words said over and over while conscious of the rhythm of your breathing, until the mind is clear and you can enter into silence. One of my favorites is a paraphrase of Psalm 130:6, "For you alone my soul in silence waits."

Presence

Now you are ready to spend time with God. In the beginning this will be comprised of paying attention and listening. First, practice receptive awareness (strive to become conscious of God's presence); second, focused attention (give your life and love to God); third, trustful openness (be in expectation); and fourth, directed energy (long for a deepened relationship with God). Once you have learned to be present and attentive to God, you can do other things together that will enhance your relationship. More about that later.

Journaling

Experiences are important, but they gain value only after we reflect on them. Maintaining a spiritual journal, therefore, is helpful. A spiritual journal is not a diary, a record of what you did. It is rather a record of what you experienced, not simply a recounting of your prayer activity. Our spiritual exercises are means, not ends. For example, we are to spend time with God rather than with the Bible. A spiritual journal is an honest record of our experiences with God, when, for example, we meditate on the scriptures, and reflections on these experiences in the form of insights and implications for our life. I find that the best way to do this is to make my entries in the form of conversations with God.

Spiritual Friends

We all need someone with whom to talk about our spiritual lives. A spiritual friend is another Christian who travels with us on our spiritual pilgrimage, listening to us, affirming us, helping us to clarify our thoughts and feelings, and when necessary, confronting us. A spiritual friend will keep us focused on our spiritual experiences and help us avoid engaging in abstract theological discourse or discussing devotional activities. Such conversations may be difficult at first. Most of us have been brought up to believe that our inner lives and feelings are private. We have been taught that we do not need help in relating to God. Many of us may find it difficult to trust another with such personal information. Preachers and teachers may find it difficult to be fully honest about spiritual matters. We, after all, are supposed to have healthy, mature relationships with God.

Spiritual friends are not to have causes or expectations for us. They are not to desire particular results, feel the need to give answers or draw conclusions for us, or encourage a dependency relationship based on wanting to help us. A spiritual friend is a sensitive, caring, open, flexible person of faith and prayer who listens well and maintains confidentiality.

Lectio Divina

Once we have established our time with God, we are ready to engage in activities with God that will enhance that relationship. In chapter 5, on ways of being spiritual, we discussed a host of different ways in which persons with various personalities might do this, but the most important and central activity is the discipline of the divine reading or praying of the scriptures. The Holy Scriptures are the Word of God in that God inspired their human authors and because God still speaks to us through them. The scriptures provide us with a doorway into an experience of God and a test of that experience. The scriptures are the Christian's primary means for developing a relationship with God. The Holy Spirit guides us into an encounter with God through the scriptures.

Christians need both to study and to pray the scriptures. Study involves us in an intellectual quest for meaning and understanding, but it can provide us only with knowledge about God. The praying of scripture involves us in an intuitive quest for meaning and understanding, which can lead us into an experience of God and aid us in developing a living relationship with God. The study is necessary but not sufficient. For example, if you are preparing to pray the story of the Good Samaritan, it is helpful to know that had the priest or the Levite approached the body lying beside the road and discovered him dead, they would, by religious law, never again have been able to practice their vocation in the Temple or make a living. They had everything to lose. The Samaritan, by contrast, had nothing to lose. In this case, when we pray the scriptures it would be better for us to identify with the priest, for all of us have something that we are not willing to sacrifice, no matter how right an action might be. All of us need to work at getting to the point where we have nothing to lose.

Nevertheless, study as we know it is not always the best aid for preparing to pray the scriptures. Only since the nineteenth century have we believed that the scriptures can be interpreted like any other book and that they have but one meaning that was in the mind of the author and which can be discovered through the historical-critical method. Earlier Christians assumed that scripture could have multiple meanings. They were aware that sometimes the meaning of a passage is obvious and relevant, but sometimes it is not. When that was the case, one of three methods of interpretation was used: the allegorical method focused on faith and what the community of faith is to be; the tropological focused on love and how the Christian is called to live; the anagogical focused on hope and what the Christian is to live for.

As an example, consider Psalm 137, in which the writer longs for a return to Jerusalem and would like God to destroy the Edomites and dash the heads of their children against the rocks. Most of us do not have any great longing to go to Jerusalem. We do not know any Edomites, and we have been taught to love our enemies and not to murder their children. The meaning, then, of this psalm for our lives is not self-evident. But if we turn Jerusalem into our life in a community of faith (allegory) or a faithful soul (tropology) or God's reign in its fullness (anagogy), it might have more meaning. In any case, the Edomites can become anyone or anything external or internal to us that is getting in the way of our reaching those ends.

Using this method of interpretive study, we can also find new meanings and relevance for passages we know well. Consider, for example, the parable of the sower, or what I have renamed "the prodigal farmer." What if we turn it into a parable about how we are to abide in God's reign until it comes in its fullness? What if we make the seed our lives and contrast living a life under our control, in which the seed is carefully planted, watered, and fertilized, with a life in which we give up control and, casting our lives to the wind, trust God? Of course, we will experience being "eaten up," "scorched," and even "dying," but we will also know abundant life. Now our parable has become a call to give up trying to control our lives, to trust in God and follow in the way of the cross, knowing that our sorrow will be turned into joy and our death into life.

Having studied our text, we are now ready to pray it, a process that involves four steps:

1. *Lectio* (Reading). Read the passage actively, that is, read it over and over slowly until you can reproduce it without the text in front of you, if it is a story, or until a word or phrase or image emerges as significant. It sometimes helps to read the passage aloud or to read from two translations, for example, the New Revised Standard Version and a dynamic, equivalent translation such as the Revised New English Bible. This sort of reading may be difficult at first, especially when the passage is familiar. But reading familiar texts slowly and actively can produce new revelations. In any case, read the text as if it were something with which you are entirely unfamiliar. Bring an openness to the text, and let whatever may happen between you and it occur. Give up control over the text. You may be surprised by what it says to you or what images or words surface for you in this reading.

2. *Meditatio* (Meditation). This second step calls for creativity. You are to enter fully into the text, let it engage you completely, and personally experience it. This involves engaging in an intuitive way of thinking and knowing, using the imagination. Stories are easy. You can enter into a story, be present to it, become one of the characters, and the like. You can become Bartimaeus, the blind beggar (Mark 10:46–52). God asks you, "What do you want me to do for you?" Tell God about your blindness (your lack of faith, your inability to see life and, especially, your life through the eyes of God). Experience what it would be like and what it would cost you if you were able to see, experience your reluctance to be healed and the joy of healing.

Or imagine an experience that is conveyed by the text. For example, Ezekiel 34:11–16 images God as the Good Shepherd. Take that image and go back to a time in your life in which you were loved, cared for, healed, fed, nurtured, nourished, protected, saved, brought home, and in your imagination experience, bathe in that grace again.

Or let a phrase surface, such as "Have mercy on me, O God" (Ps. 51:1), and turn it into a centering prayer. Or take a phrase such as "I have called you by name, you are mine" (Isa. 43:1) and focus on the feelings that this phrase engenders and in your imagination enter fully into these feelings. Or enter into a letter of Paul's as if it were a letter to you. For example, Paul writes, "Do not claim to be wiser than you are" (Rom. 12:16). Permit to surface the faces of those whose thoughts you ignore or believe foolish and listen to them as if they have something to say to you.

Or take a canticle such as Isaiah 12:2–6 and, using your imagination, compose your own canticle on what God has done for you; or in your imagination, dance a psalm. Or take a passage from the Song of Songs (5:2–6, for example) and reverse the usual understanding. For example, make God the bride and you become the groom. Imagine that when God is about to enter into intimate lovemaking with you, your fear of this intimacy causes you to turn your back on God. The examples can go on, but entering into the text so that you can experience it is the essential part of this step.

3. *Oratio* (Prayer). In this case, prayer is understood as a conversation with God using one's imagination. Many of us in our culture have permitted our imaginations to atrophy. If you discover that this is the case, you will need to practice using it by engaging in dance, painting, sculpture, or music. What you are doing in this time of prayer is reflecting with God on your experience; you are discussing with God the meaning of that experience and trying to name insights

concerning your relationship with God. Even more impor-tant, you are striving, with God's help, to name the implica-tions for that relationship. Some find this step is most easily done in writing. The key to this step is to arrive at implica-tions and the awareness of what grace or graces you will need if you are to enhance and enliven your spiritual life.

4. *Contemplatio* (Contemplation). In this case, contempla-tion is a process of opening yourself to receive and experience the grace you have requested so that you might deepen your relationship with God. To do this you need to empty your conscious, controlling mind, give up control, wait patiently, and watch expectantly for God's action in your life. When this is completed, it will be helpful to make a record of your praying of the scriptures in your journal. State what you read, on what concerns you dwelt, what you experienced, what insights and implications resulted, and what graces you received.

A Disciplined Life

To summarize, we all need to develop a life lived in a rhythm of daily prayer, study, work, and leisure. We need to worship in community and alone regularly. We need to learn to live with greater simplicity and with deep compassion. We need to live self-critical lives to ensure that our spiritual life (our relationship with God) is resulting in a moral life (a healthy relation with our true self, all other persons, and the whole of creation). Most of all, when faced with the difficul-ties of life, we need to maintain stability in our exterior life and focus on change in our interior life. The spiritual life nec-essarily comes first. If that is the case, we each will need to develop spiritual discipline to sustain it. I hope this chapter has helped you to do that.[1]

Conclusion

In a moving letter addressed to Gordon Lang, archbishop of Canterbury from 1928–42, the Anglican laywoman and spiritual writer Evelyn Underhill wrote to the bishops assembled at Lambeth that what the church needed most was to call the church's teachers and preachers to a greater interiority and the cultivation of their spiritual lives. At ninety years of age, she was convinced that the real failures, difficulties, and weaknesses of the church were spiritual and that the church's deepest need was spiritual renewal, first of those who taught and preached and through them for all the people of God.

Karl Rahner, the Jesuit priest-theologian, in what reads like entries in a spiritual journal, writes a letter to God.[1] In it, he brings his daily life before God and discusses the long days and tedious hours that are filled with all sorts of activities but not with God. He ponders what will become of him when he dies and there is no more daily routine. He acknowledges that the one thing necessary for life is a relationship with God. Further, he is aware that if he can lose God in everything he does, he can find God in everything he does. He therefore concludes that he must, with God's help, seek God amid the routine of daily life. Thus he lays his routine before God and asks for God's most ordinary and exalted gift, already offered: the gift of God's presence and love. So must all of us who preach and teach.

Such an awareness and action is described beautifully in Teresa of Avila's *Interior Castle*.[2] Teresa, a sixteenth-century "doctor of the church" and holy woman, reminds us that we human beings are the house of the Holy Spirit and that in our search for God we find God already residing within us, closer than our breath, waiting for us to journey together. Our spiritual journey begins as we enter the rooms of our soul and find God already present. We offer to make our soul a home for God so that together we might grow into an ever-deepening and loving relationship, which is the purpose of human life.

Prayer provides the means by which our human soul has intercourse with God. It includes all the work done by God through, in, and with the souls that have given themselves to God in prayer. God is spirit and we, God's children, are spiritual creatures. God is never far from us, indeed, God dwells within each of us, and in prayer we become aware of God's continuous presence and activity, calling, guiding, and empowering us for life and redeeming our lives when we do not hear the call and accept God's guidance and power.

Preachers and teachers whose lives are centered in prayer, that is, whose relationship with God comes first, will always communicate the gospel, because they have been enabled to reveal in their personal lives its attractiveness and transforming power.

Not only are the spiritual life and prayer the primary obligation of all preachers and teachers but also the only condition under which their work can be properly done. It is the preachers and teachers whose spiritual lives are deep and strong whose ministries are also deep and strong. I am convinced, by my own experience, that the heart of the vocation of preachers and teachers is prayer. Only if we experience the mysterious attraction of God will we be able to impart it to others.

The hidden foundation of that life to which we have been called as preachers and teachers is prayer. All human life has two dimensions, our relationship to God on which we depend and our relationship with those we teach or to whom we preach. Without the first, we cannot adequately perform the second. It is not that preachers or teachers are any different from other Christians, it is just that their calling is to model the life necessary and possible for all.

Evelyn Underhill, in an address to teachers and preachers in 1927, describes how she was present at some sheepdog trials.[3] She suggests that teachers and preachers are called to help the shepherd of souls, Jesus, to deal with the lambs and young sheep of his flock, just as the sheepdog works with the flock. She goes on to explain how those sheepdogs gave her insights into the pastoral work of teachers and preachers. They were helping the shepherd deal with a lot of very active sheep and lambs, persuading them to go into the right pastures, keeping them from running down the wrong paths. They did it, interestingly, not by barking, fuss, ostentatious authority, or any kind of busy behavior. The best dog she saw never barked once; but he spent an astonishing amount of time sitting perfectly still, looking at the shepherd. The communion of spirit between them was perfect. They worked as a unit. Neither of them seemed anxious or in a hurry. Neither was committed to a rigid plan; they were always content to wait patiently. The dog was the docile and faithful agent of another mind with whom the dog was in communion. The dog used his whole intelligence and intuition, but always in obedience to the master's directive will, and was ever prompt at self-effacement. The little mountain sheep the dog had to deal with were amazingly tiresome, experts in doubling and twisting and going in the wrong way. The dog went steadily on with the work, his tail never ceasing to wag. This meant that the dog's relation to the shepherd was the center of the dog's life, and because of that, the dog enjoyed doing this job with the sheep. The dog did not bother about the trouble or get discouraged with the apparent results. The dog had transcended mere dogginess. The dog's actions were dictated by a power beyond self. The dog was the agent of the shepherd, working for a scheme that was the shepherd's and the whole of which the dog could not grasp; and it was just that which was the source of the delightedness, the eagerness, and also the discipline with which the dog worked. The dog, Underhill reminds us, would not have kept that peculiar and intimate relationship unless the dog had sat down and looked at the shepherd first, for a long time. So it will be for every one of us who accepts the call to preach and teach the gospel of Jesus Christ, the true shepherd.

Though my roots were Protestant, within the Reformed tradition, as an Anglo-Catholic Episcopalian my disposition is today more toward the Orthodox and Roman Catholic spiritual traditions. Nevertheless, I remain indebted to a Reformed spirituality that taught me to long for an experience of God. Today, all Christians are seeking a deeper experiential relationship with God and a faith founded on firsthand experience.

While I wrote this book for all Christians, I was invited to do so by a press that is in the Reformed tradition. I am grateful and, therefore, quote from John Calvin: the reason for prayer is "that our hearts may be fired with a zealous and burning desire ever to seek, love, and serve God."[4] Also, I want to recommend Howard Rice's fine book *Reformed Spirituality*. In it he reminds us, "The spiritual life, the pursuit of God's presence, the longing for a personal relationship with God are only a human response to the divine invitation. . . . It is God's prompting that initiates the spiritual pilgrimage."[5] May all of us who have been called to preach and teach hear and accept that call.

Notes

Chapter 1: Exploring the Spiritual Life

1. Kenneth Leech, *The Eye of the Storm: Living Spiritually in the Real World* (San Francisco: HarperCollins, 1992), 201.

2. Paul Wadell, *Friendship and the Moral Life* (Notre Dame, Ind.: University of Notre Dame Press, 1989), chap. 2.

Chapter 2: Preaching and Teaching in a New Day

1. Andrew Louth, *Discerning the Mystery: An Essay on the Nature of Theology* (Oxford: Clarendon Press, 1983).

2. Urban Holmes, *Ministry and the Imagination* (New York: Seabury Press, 1976), 98.

3. Amos Wilder, *Theopoetic: Theology and the Religious Imagination* (Philadelphia: Fortress Press, 1976), 1.

4. Ibid., 2.

5. Edward Robinson, *The Language of Mystery* (London: SCM Press, 1987).

6. Parker Palmer, *To Know As We Are Known: The Spirituality of Teaching* (San Francisco: Harper & Row, 1983).

7. Maria Harris, *Teaching and the Religious Imagination* (San Francisco: Harper & Row, 1987), chap. 2.

Chapter 3: The Spirituality of Preachers and Teachers

1. Alan Jones, *Exploring Spiritual Direction* (New York: Seabury Press, 1982), 23–25.

2. Graham Greene, *Dr. Fisher of Geneva, or the Bomb Party* (New York: Simon & Schuster, 1980), 192–94.

3. Walker Percy, *The Second Coming* (New York: Farrar, Straus & Giroux, 1980), 45.

Chapter 4: The Spirituality of Preaching and Teaching

1. Benjamin Jacobs, *The Sunday School Teacher's Guide* (New York: The Female Union Society for the Growth of the Sabbath School, 1876), 38.

2. L. F. Senabaugh, *The Modern Sunday School* (New York: Hunt & Eaton, 1887), 39.

3. Alice Walker, *Revolutionary Petunias and Other Poems* (New York: Harcourt Brace & Company, 1970), 11.

4. Parker Palmer, *To Know As We Are Known: The Spirituality of Teaching* (San Francisco: Harper & Row, 1983).

Chapter 5: Various Ways of Living Spiritually

1. Urban Holmes, *A History of Spirituality* (New York: Seabury Press, 1980).

2. See, for example, Chester Michael and Marie Norrisey, *Prayer and Temperament* (Charlottesville, Va.: Open Door Press, 1984); and Charles Keating, *Who We Are Is How We Pray* (Mystic, Conn.: Twenty-third Publications, 1987).

3. Ibid.

Chapter 6: Developing a Spiritual Discipline

1. For other ideas, see the following: Thomas Greene, (Notre Dame, Ind.: Ave Maria Press, 1977); Andre Louf, *Teach Us to Pray* (Cambridge, Mass.: Cowley, 1992); Nancy Roth, *The Breath of God* (Cambridge, Mass.: Cowley, 1990); Herbert Slade, *Explorations into Contemplative Prayer* (New York: Paulist Press, 1973); Jeremy Taylor, *Holy Living* (Orleans, Mass.: Paraclete Press, 1993); Francis Vanderwall, *Water in the Wilderness* (New York: Paulist Press, 1985).

Conclusion

1. Karl Rahner, *Prayers for a Lifetime* (New York: Crossroad, 1989), 89–97.

2. Teresa of Avila, *Interior Castle* (New York: Paulist Press, 1979).

3. Evelyn Underhill, *Life as Prayer* (Harrisburg, Pa.: Morehouse Press, 1946), 157–58.

4. John Calvin, *Institutes of the Christian Religion* (Philadelphia: Westminster Press, 1960), vol. 2, p. 852.

5. Howard Rice, *Reformed Spirituality* (Louisville, Ky.: Westminster/John Knox Press, 1991), 197.